"I Love You, Too!"

"I Love You, Too!"

WOODROW WIRSIG

M. EVANS & COMPANY   NEW YORK

Library of Congress Cataloging-in-Publication Data

Wirsig, Woodrow.

I love you too! / Woodrow Wirsig.
p.   cm.
ISBN 0-87131-616-1   : $18.95
1. Wirsig, Jane—Health.   2. Alzheimer's disease—Patients—
United States—Biography.   I. Title.
RC523.W57W57   1990
362.1'96831'0092—dc20

[B]   90-3269
CIP

M. Evans and Company, Inc.
216 East 49 Street
New York, New York 10017

Manufactured in the United States of America

2 4 6 8 9 7 5 3 1

This is the story of our search . . . of our hope and love. It's the story of my wife, Jane, and me in our search for ways to diminish the ravages of Alzheimer's disease, Parkinson's, strokes, and spinal infarction—ending with the effects of the new experimental, unapproved drug THA for Alzheimer's.

It's a story of never-ending hope against continuous disappointment—until THA. It's a love story. It may be of some hope and help to those who love a handicapped person.

Contents

"I Love You, Too!"

1

Is Hope Enough?

My battle with the Food and Drug Administration dragged on for four weeks. To me, it was bitter and disheartening. Statements were made, then denied. People lied. Minds changed. Underneath it all were envy and bureaucratic intransigence. After a decade of sorrow, on the verge of real help, I was discouraged to the point of giving up.

Suddenly, at 6 A.M. California time, a call from Washington, D.C., woke me. A voice, clear and authoritative, came over the line:

"Mr. Wirsig? This is Frank Young, commissioner of the FDA. Can you hear me all right? I'm calling from my car phone. . . ."

Commissioner Young was calling to tell me the way had been cleared for my wife, Jane, to receive the new THA treatment for Alzheimer's disease. She could now become a patient of Dr. William K. Summers, in Arcadia, California, where more than a dozen victims of Alzheimer's disease had shown unusual improvement with the THA drug.

A surge of hope rose in me once again. At last, maybe this time we had found something that could really help Jane. . . .

My wife, Jane, and I have been fighting to save her life. From the beginning I knew it was a tough, probably losing struggle. But hope kept us going—until it seemed that hope itself, for its own sake perhaps, could make a difference.

In her soft, plucky way, Jane has been fighting to live—and she will keep on, whatever happens. We'll both see to that.

In so many ways, the battle itself is a victory. As we take our walks, she consciously enjoys the flowers and lovely days.

"Isn't it beautiful?" she will exclaim at a scene of flowers and a white picket fence.

We play games. And she spots babies in strollers with a smile. "Isn't he cute?" she will say.

As I look back, I realize we've had these last ten years of being together in ways we would never have experienced during healthier circumstances. Almost every waking moment is, in itself, a pleasing one.

We walk hand in hand, her hand eagerly clasping mine in anticipation of the adventure ahead. I kiss her often, on the street, in the elevator, as I'm feeding her, telling her again . . . and again . . . how much I love her.

She looks back at me with knowing eyes and, from time to time, can say "I love you."

These are some of the reasons for writing this story of Jane. I wish I could capture better the true, complete essence of this remarkable woman: brilliant student . . . independent thinker . . . exceptional professional writer . . . successful executive . . . loving wife and mother.

There was a time when Jane handled everything well. Cum laude at Vassar, she won all the top prizes at the Graduate School of Journalism at Columbia University. Graduating at twenty-two, she went right to work writing CBS's biggest news show, the "Morning News Roundup." She wrote with a smooth narrative style, astutely organizing facts and thoughts. She called in such correspondents as Edward R. Murrow, Charles Collingwood, William Shirer. Jane sold the first short story she ever wrote. Then she decided to marry me and we reared three sons. When they entered high school, Jane went back to work. She started the Publications Division of Educational Testing Service. Later, she became executive director of all information services. Finally, she was promoted to corporate secretary of ETS. Somehow, she found time to serve on a Boy Scouts' Council Board and was one of only two women ever to be chairman of the Princeton, New Jersey, Chamber of Commerce. Above all, she has been a loving wife. She has made me happy for forty-eight years.

Perhaps this story can be helpful, even useful, to those millions of family members whose loved ones suffer from the dreadful Alzheimer's disease. As my readers will plainly see, this is not a "how to" book on caring for a victim. Many such books are available.

There may be other stories like this one, which tries to express feelings—not only the sorrow, the dashed hopes, the despair of seeing a loved one slowly fading away, but the feelings of love, too, love deepened and sharply etched as never before. Surely there is such a story in the heart of anyone who loves an Alzheimer's victim.

I believe—it's almost a fierce belief—that if one loves a mother or father, a wife or husband, then there are ways to help make the last days have meaning. The ways Jane and I found may help someone else understand the dimensions of his own love and express what each moment means.

Nothing, of course, is all sugar and sweetness. There

have been grim moments in these past few years. I often feel overwhelming sorrow and despair at slowly losing Jane. That said, however, I still enjoy being with her.

I'm delighted to see her smile and exclaim over babies and little children. Passersby always bring a smile and hello from her. Quickly she says "thank you" whenever it's appropriate. As we walk slowly along the sidewalks in Princeton, Jane's short, mincing steps becoming ever shorter and slower, I am at peace with my world. And I feel that Jane is happy.

How long does Jane have? How many more days, weeks, even years do we have together? I don't know. Jane seems to be strong, physically. She looks good. Her friends remark on how young she appears. It is the tenth year of her affliction.

But the messages from her brain to her muscles are slower, become increasingly tangled and interrupted. I'm struggling in every possible way to preserve what she has, to flatten out her decline, to keep her happy and contented and enjoying what she still understands.

Yet complications will inevitably set in. The day will come for feeding Jane by tube. At any time she might aspirate food into her lungs, precipitating deadly pneumonia. Kidneys may fail. There will be that terrible time, doctors say, when Jane will no longer know me. The disease is relentless.

Long ago, however, I came to a conclusion. We would continue to fight, as we have in the past, until the last breath. We don't know how much the brain retains or what it can recognize, even if there is no response. I will always—always—assume that somewhere deep in her subconscious, Jane will know my kisses, my touch, my words "I love you."

I will be there, kissing her, telling her again—and again—how much I love her, holding her against the coming night.

Until then, however, we are two against this disease.

We will read and learn, we'll watch for new developments as we have in years past. We'll try promising avenues. We'll keep on trying to help find the cause, the prevention, hopefully the cure.

Hope may not be enough, but it is all we have.

2

Our Battle Begins

It was the day of the "shower cap." It was the day Jane and I began the fight for her life. She was only sixty, that summer of 1980.

At breakfast, Jane said, "I must get my shower cap done," her hands patting her hair in place.

"Shower cap?" I asked. "Why the shower cap?" As usual, I was deep in the morning paper and only half aware of what Jane was saying.

"No, darling," she said. "I have to get a shampoo and set."

I suddenly felt chilled. With an awful clarity other instances came rushing back into my mind.

There was the time a few weeks ago when she was working on our accounts. Suddenly, in exasperation, she slapped her hands to her hips and declared, "I must be losing my mind." She had forgotten how to add.

Then I realized that she no longer wore makeup—and I knew that I had been noticing this for many months, but assumed it was some naturalistic fad that Princeton women were going through. I couldn't remember when she had stopped.

Slow to alarm, but finally worried enough to check on it, I arranged for Jane to have an appointment with her physician, Dr. David Fulmer, a member of the prestigious Princeton Medical Group. I played golf regularly with his architect father.

So as not to frighten Jane, I suggested that it was time for her to have her regular physical examination. She readily agreed.

I'll always remember my talk with Dave Fulmer after he saw Jane.

"Woody," he said in a worried voice, "I never realized it before. But Jane does have difficulty remembering some things. I tried her on some of the simple tests—counting backward, for instance. She can't. We ought to have her see a neurologist."

Did Jane know what was happening to her?

I don't know.

In a general sense, she knew that something was different as long ago as 1977. Friends tell me that she would invite a staff member to lunch and be unable to add the check or figure out the tip. Casually, she would slide it over to her companion and say, "Would you add this up for me and put down the right tip? Then I'll sign it."

The time must have come when she felt she was losing her hold on her job. I'll never know the extent of her concern, her fears, her confusion. She rarely talked about such matters because she was rarely troubled by such matters.

One evening, after we had finished eating dinner, had put the dishes into the dishwasher, and were reading the papers in front of the TV, she turned to me and said, calmly but with feeling:

"Wood, I don't know what's happening to me. I feel so

discouraged about my work . . . my job . . . my marriage. . . ."

I got up from my chair and knelt beside her and took her in my arms.

"Darling," I said, kissing her again and again as I so often do, "I love you more than anything in the world. I always have—and always will."

She smiled and sighed.

"You've made me happy all of our life together," I said. "Maybe I'm not a very good husband. There's a lot I could help you with. But I love you, love you, love you—and always will. You're a wonderful wife to me—a wonderful mother of our sons."

Again she smiled and kissed me.

"We'll make it together," I said. "Whatever it is, whatever the problem, we'll make out all right."

Then I reviewed with her her work, her job. At the time I didn't suspect that the quality of her work was slipping, or had slipped. I just knew she was the best staff member Educational Testing Service ever had in the jobs she held.

She sighed, responded sweetly, and seemed relieved.

In retrospect, now, as I recall again and again and again the times when I could have been a better husband, the remorse engulfing me, I will always remember that evening . . . our talk, and my opportunity to assure her and reassure her of my love for her. At times, the memory of those moments is the only thing that keeps me going.

Does Jane know about her illness?

I think she does not know. I believe she does not.

Once, with blinding clarity and understanding, Jane momentarily seemed to understand what was happening.

A look of terror crossed her face. She turned to me, almost in panic, and asked, "What's wrong with me?"

At that moment, I took her in my arms, held her, kissed her, and in my most persuasive tones assured her that nothing was wrong with her, that everything was going to be all right. I rationalized my answer by asking myself what good could come from letting her know about the disease. While she might forget it in a few moments, her fear and panic for those few moments would be terrible for her to bear.

Almost all of the time Jane seems serenely confident that all is well with her and the world . . . that whatever is being done to her, or happening, is normal and appropriate.

I like to think, then, that Jane has not known, and does not know, of her disease and what it is doing to her.

But of course I'll never be sure.

3

What the Neurologist Said

When the day came for our appointment with the neu-rologist, a few days following our meeting with Dr. Fulmer, Jane was calm. I've always admired, even loved, her serenity, especially during those times I was tense. I had a foreboding, however.

The doctor asked me to sit in on the interview. She, of course, didn't mind at all. She seemed to regard it as just another meeting—the kind of meeting she had attended thousands of times. I wish it had been routine.

As he proceeded, I realized what the doctor was doing. He was testing Jane's memory. He wanted to find out how she handled some of the simplest abstractions.

"Jane," the doctor would say, "count backward for me from 97."

She tried but got mixed up.

"What year is this, Jane?" the doctor asked.

She could not answer.

Jane tried to respond to all the questions, but found them difficult. At times, she became slightly exasperated with herself, knowing that she knew the answers to his questions—but unable to get quite the right answers at the moment.

The doctor sighed. "Before I draw any conclusions," he said, "I'd like to get a CAT scan of Jane's brain."

At that, Jane looked questioningly at me. I smiled and held her hand, saying as reassuringly as I could that it was nothing but a complicated X ray. She seemed relieved.

Driving to the hospital in New Brunswick was like any other outing for us. Jane took it in stride as if we were going to the golf course.

Several days later, we met with the doctor to discuss the CAT scan results. He fidgeted in his chair and couldn't seem to look straight at me. I felt chilled.

"My own wife," the doctor began, "is getting more forgetful these days. So I've prescribed an aspirin a day for her. I'm sure it will help her memory."

I waited, my apprehension growing. I knew this wasn't the real message.

"The CAT scan is inconclusive," he said. Jane sat there with me, but tended to tune out statements that weren't directed at her. "I notice some enlargement of the ventricles. This might mean that she is suffering from some early form of hydrocephalus."

He saw the hope in my eyes and nodded.

"We can usually handle those things," he went on, "even by running a drainage tube down into her neck. . . ." He paused.

"And—it could be Alzheimer's, of course," he said, trying to be casual. "I'm really a neurosurgeon. I suggest that you have Jane see a neurologist. In the meantime, you might start her taking an aspirin a day."

Alzheimer's! I'd heard the name. Somehow I associated it with memory loss. And there was something else, something I couldn't put my finger on, some dreaded fact that it kept getting worse. But I hadn't read enough to know—only enough to be worried.

Dave Fulmer suggested we see a neurologist whom he admired and liked, Dr. John O'Brien, of Columbia Presbyterian in New York. That was fine with me, and Jane was unquestioning. We got the appointment quickly, which surprised me.

Dr. O'Brien examined Jane alone, while I waited in the outer office. When he met with me, his face was a mask. He spoke in a flat tone, without emotion.

"I'm convinced that Jane has Alzheimer's disease," he said. Then he stopped and waited.

I hesitated a moment, then asked the question he was anticipating. "What can we do, doctor?"

He shook his head slightly. "Nothing, I'm afraid," he said. "We don't know what causes Alzheimer's. And there's no cure. And I'm afraid it's progressive. . . ." His voice trailed off.

I sat stunned. During the past few weeks I'd begun reading all I could find on Alzheimer's disease. Remorselessly degenerative, the disease took victims' memories, then their abilities to talk, to recognize loved ones, then body functions—and then, usually, resulted in an early death. But I had only begun reading. . . .

I determined to fight, as I knew Jane would if she knew. While she heard the words, in our conversations, she didn't seem to associate them with herself. It seemed to me that she was placidly going through the motions simply to satisfy me. And I felt that I should keep everything from her. I thought: What if I told her? Could it help? What could she do? She was already becoming severely limited. To me, it seemed that she would only suffer horrible fear.

So, Jane and I continued the fight—and, in a way, I gave up at the same time. It's hard even for me to understand. I was determined to do everything I possibly could, yet I understood that thus far it was hopeless. Perhaps by "giving up" I meant that we did not begin frantically rushing after rumored "cures." I decided I would read everything, explore everything, especially on the cutting edge of the problem, and go through experimental programs—if there were any. Otherwise, we'd try just to live the best we could, being together as much as possible.

I would try to keep her comfortable and make her happy.

When I mentioned the results of our meeting with Dr. O'Brien to my long-time friend and internist, Dr. Leonard Stone, in New York, Leonard expressed his own deep sorrow. But he, too, is a fighter. He would not give up, either.

"Woody," he said, "let me take a look at Jane. Maybe it's just her anemia flaring up again. You know that severe anemia can give symptoms very similar to Alzheimer's symptoms."

Again, I felt hope. Perhaps that was it. Jane had always been anemic. At times, when she hadn't been examined as frequently as she should, her anemia would become severe and fatigue would drag her down.

After Leonard had given Jane a thorough physical examination, he called me at home. His voice was urgent.

"My God, Woody," he began. "Jane has lost a lot of blood— maybe a quart!"

Fear gripped me. "Is it bad?" I asked.

"Didn't you notice it—in her stools? Anyway, she has a severe problem. We should get on it right away. What could have happened?"

"I don't know," I said. I was going through some complicated and mixed feelings of my own. Serious as the blood loss might be, possibly *that* could be Jane's problem. And if so, *that* could be fixed.

"We haven't been doing anything different," I went on. "Except that since our talk with the neurosurgeon who told us about giving his wife an aspirin a day, I've been giving Jane an aspirin a day."

Leonard swore. "That's it," he said. I felt he could have

killed me over the phone. If it could have done any good I'd have let him.

Immediately Leonard put Jane through an X-ray procedure. He discovered that she was suffering from a bleeding duodenal ulcer. He put her on Tagamet. Within a matter of weeks *that* problem was cleared up.

But her memory did not return.

"I think we ought to have a second opinion, Woody," Leonard said. "I'd like Jane to see a great old neurologist, Morris Bender. He's still one of the best."

I found Dr. Bender to be a bustling, energetic, slightly portly man who looked more like a corporate president than a doctor. He was businesslike and forthright in the way he approached his examination of Jane. The way he handled her was almost brusque. In a way, I was almost relieved. He gave me the impression that when he got through we'd surely know. We'd *really* know for sure.

Dr. Bender put Jane through all the mental tests I'd listened to several times before. But he also took Jane into an examining room and put her through a physical routine.

"Please walk along this line for me, Mrs. Wirsig," Dr. Bender asked. Jane wavered. She couldn't walk in a straight line.

"Close your eyes, please," Dr. Bender asked, "and point to your nose with your left hand." With her right hand, Jane pointed to her chin.

Dr. Bender checked her reflexes, had her sit down, stand up, cross her legs, and other simple movements. He watched her intently, studying every move.

This was different from the other examinations. I could only suspect he was checking her level of physical coordination—how her muscles responded to directions from her brain.

When he was through, Jane and I sat at his desk waiting for his verdict. I couldn't help thinking he looked like a businessman about to address a board of directors.

"It's Alzheimer's disease," he said. "I'm sure of it. I'm

sorry, but that's it. And there isn't a thing we can do about it."

My heart seemed to stop, he was so final. I looked at Jane and saw that she was looking at me. Her expression was quizzical, but certainly not fearful. She still didn't connect his words with herself.

What now? As I led Jane out of Dr. Bender's office, the chill of the fall air hit us. I realized winter was coming. I disliked the cold and dark of winter days.

The time ahead looked terribly dismal and bleak.

At that moment, I remember thinking that at least Jane didn't have cancer. She wouldn't suffer that kind of pain. Perhaps she wouldn't really suffer at all. That, at least, would be a blessing.

By this time I'd read almost everything I could get my hands on about Alzheimer's disease. Experts believed that the neurotransmitter acetylcholine, a chemical that flowed between nerve endings, was missing in Alzheimer's patients. This resulted in their brain cells dying at such a rate that they clumped together in "plaques." Nerve fibers became tangled into what they called neurofibrilary tangles. These changes continued and increased remorselessly, gradually depriving the victim of memory, the use of the body, ending too soon in death. No wonder Jane sometimes sounded like a switchboard with all the lines mixed up.

After reading all the theories, which never proved out in the tests, I was even more discouraged.

"We tried giving people lecithin until it came out of their ears," said Leonard Stone. "Perhaps some of it turned to choline in the brain. If so, it wasn't enough to make a particle of difference."

Was there any kind of a drug that would pass the blood-brain barrier, a web of blood vessels and tissues that keeps most dangerous substances out of the brain, like Sinemet, used for Parkinson's disease victims? After all, Sinemet consisted of L-dopa, a neurotransmitter.

The answer: "They're still working on it. Nothing yet will both pass the blood-brain barrier and supplant the missing acetylcholine."

Almost everything Jane does and says evokes happy and sad feelings in me. I am happy that she's not in pain, but so despairingly sad at what is happening to her mind.

One of these sweet-sad experiences came six years after her illness began, one Christmas at the home of Elizabeth Riley, with whom we have shared Christmas eves since our sons grew up, moved away, and began holding family Christmases of their own.

That Christmas Eve, Elizabeth happened to have a hand-sewn teddy bear, with its own sweater, made carefully and lovingly by an associate who wanted Elizabeth to see that it found an appropriate home.

Elizabeth showed the teddy bear to Jane. At once Jane enfolded it in her arms as if it were a baby. Holding it tenderly, slightly rocking it back and forth, Jane began to croon loving, incoherent thoughts at the little bear, reassuring it and patting it softly, as if it were her child.

Elizabeth realized that the teddy bear's best home would be with Jane.

We named him Teddy, of course. All babies were "hims" to Jane, after raising three sons of her own. Teddy has been with us ever since.

In the morning, after I give Jane juice and vitamins, we take a walk through our home. I always tell her, "Teddy is waiting for you. Teddy loves you, you know. And he's waiting to see you."

I never know what Jane does, or doesn't, understand. But when I say "Teddy" and "Teddy loves you," her eyes light up, a smile curves her lips, and she seems to enjoy the anticipation of seeing Teddy and holding him again.

As we enter the den, the first thing I do is lead Jane to her chair and hold up Teddy.

"Here's Teddy," I say. "He's waiting to see you."

Jane always smiles, opens her arms, moves toward Teddy with crooning sounds, saying a few phrases clearly such as "Oh, isn't he sweet" or "Isn't he wonderful." She enfolds him in her arms, sits down, and holds him on her lap facing her. Then she talks to him as if he were one of her babies, expostulating sweetly in mixed-up words. She looks and sounds rational, as if inside she knows precisely what it is she's trying to say—and why.

Then she will arrange and rearrange Teddy's sweater. She will take it off, then put it back on. Often she sits and twists his ears into proper position.

There are times when Jane seems even more rational than usual. At these times, when I give Teddy to her, she will laugh, take him in her arms, and say, "Isn't he funny?" At these times, I know that she knows that Teddy is just a funny-looking little teddy bear.

4

Will Megavitamins Help?

Even though it seemed futile, I kept asking myself, "Is there anything else I can do?" Half of me wanted to give up and the other half wanted to fight. It wasn't a conflict, rather, the two feelings seemed to exist together. I could give vent to both at the same time. Most of the time, I realize, I was trying to find ways to help.

I decided, soon after her diagnosis, to take Jane to Princeton Brain-Bio, a clinic founded by Dr. Carl Pfeiffer and specializing in nutrition therapy through the use of vitamin and mineral supplements.

For many years I'd read of Dr. Pfeiffer's work. He was one of the pioneers in the use of massive doses of Vitamin C and niacin to treat schizophrenia and other forms of depression. In my mind, there was no question that Dr. Pfeiffer and his associates had enabled thousands of hospitalized schizophrenics and depressed people to go back home and lead normal lives.

I already believed in vitamins and minerals for myself. From reading everything I could find about vitamins, I had become convinced that these supplements, used carefully, couldn't hurt—and just might do some good.

My first contact with Vitamin E had come through reading in *Time* magazine, about forty-five years ago, about the experiments of the Shute brothers, in Canada. Both doctors believed that Vitamin E helped keep muscles healthy; they claimed success in the use of Vitamin E for victims of heart attacks.

At the time, for some reason or other, I had a stiff neck. I decided to try Vitamin E. And I've been taking it regularly ever since. Some people say that I look and act much younger than my seventy-four years—and I guess I do. If so, I ascribe it to my taking vitamins and minerals.

As I made the appointment with Dr. Pfeiffer, I was prepared to react positively to whatever he might say about Alzheimer's disease and Jane's problem. I also was impressed by what he'd done for some friends of mine—one in particular, a sixty-nine-year-old woman who had had a heart attack and been bedridden ever since, unresponsive to treatment at some of the world's best heart clinics. She went to Dr. Pfeiffer, who studied her body chemistry. He eliminated one trace mineral from her body—and within six weeks she was playing golf again, and has been playing regularly ever since.

Jane and I entered the Brain-Bio clinic and began a simple process—first, a urine sample, then a sample of Jane's blood. Then we met Dr. Pfeiffer, whose snow-white hair, rosy cheeks, and big smile reminded us of our ideal Santa Claus.

"We'll try," he began, "to give Jane three or four more years of good, conscious living." And he proceeded to work out the first part of a vitamin-mineral regimen for her.

"Let's hope," I murmured as we headed for his vitamin counter.

Dr. Pfeiffer's approach upsets some patients who are more comfortable with the orthodox system—examination, diagnosis, then prescription. Dr. Pfeiffer asks patients to fill out a questionnaire, then talks to them in his office. Then, before the blood analysis is in, and with only the preliminary work on urine, to disclose the presence or absence of sugar, he writes out an initial prescription of vitamins and minerals.

Some of these supplements are part of his basic prescription for everyone, convinced as he is that everybody is deficient in C, B complex, E, and so on. For Jane there were more: lecithin, niacin, and a group of other vitamins and minerals designed to do specific jobs in her body.

Did it help Jane? Does it make much difference? There's no direct way to tell, of course.

I do know this, however: Today, nine years later, Jane looks fifteen years younger than her age of sixty-eight. Many exclaim at how young, how vibrant, she looks. I know, too, that Jane and the famous movie actress Rita Hayworth are of the same age. Both were diagnosed as having Alzheimer's disease at the same time. Both, for several years, had the same neurologist. Although I have not seen Rita for decades—not since I put her on the cover of my magazines, in fact—I understand that she has been inert and uncomprehending for years. [Since this writing, Rita Hayworth has died.]

On the other hand, Jane walks every day. She knows me, greets me with a smile and loving kiss, obviously enjoys being with me. She enjoys watching babies and little children, the flowers, beauty anywhere. I take her shopping in the supermarket, where she loves to push the cart through the aisles.

If Jane sat in the midst of a poised, sophisticated group of people, one would have difficulty singling her out as "different."

My conclusion, therefore, is that *something* has helped Jane to a considerable degree. "Something" has given her nine years of a relatively serene, happy life that she might otherwise never have known. That something *has* to be the vitamin-mineral program she's been on.

Nothing else is different.

Jane is learning to count the steps up to our bedroom, because some six years into her illness she has forgotten so much—and must learn basic actions as if she were a child. She is getting the hang of pulling up her slacks by herself. She can tuck in the shirttails of her blouse.

Now, she is conquering her fear and learning to sit down . . . to stand up . . . to step into bathtubs . . . to lie down in bed.

After each triumph she smiles in satisfaction. She's learning to use some of her brain cells that are still healthy.

As Jane struggles to hold onto some coherent life, I'm doing my best to help her. And I'm more active than I've ever been before in my life.

I'm too busy to cry.

Jane knows I love her. Now, though, I feel that I never told her often enough. Nor did I express often enough how happy she has made me during our years together. So this is the least I can do—comfort her and help her learn to use what's left of her brain.

From the beginning of Jane's illness I believed, and still believe, that the process of caring for an Alzheimer's patient can be much better than it usually is. So I decided to do a different, perhaps better, job of it. Such care leads to stress. And this stress may have contributed to my heart attack three years ago. I'm no Pollyanna, as my friends and enemies would attest, but I feel that the stress is worth it. At the very least, this is a chance to do something vital and important for someone one loves.

I decided to see if brain cells left untouched by the plaques and neurofibrillary tangles could be taught. Perhaps these cells could take on some of the tasks formerly done by cells now dead. Why not try? Why not, indeed. There was nothing to lose and possibly much to gain, even if, in the end, it was a lost battle.

Once I get past the inexpressible sorrow and into the interminable hours of showering, changing diapers, dressing, cooking meals, washing dishes, doing the laundry, shopping, and running errands, our routine has had its amusing moments.

Jane, for example, firmly and even enthusiastically counts the first seven steps on the way upstairs. But that, she evidently feels, is enough. She will not count the second seven steps up from the landing, no matter how I plead with her. So we play games. We'll ignore the first flight and concentrate on counting the second flight, which she gladly does. But does this lead to counting both flights? Not yet.

Coming downstairs involves the same learning game, only in reverse. Jane eagerly counts the first seven steps down to the landing. And she blithely ignores the second seven steps. So this has become a target—to get her to count all the steps.

Jane's slacks present a similar challenge—and reaction. Her everyday slacks are loose and bulky enough to cover her diapers comfortably. These slacks Jane will quickly, and with confidence, pull up over her hips, tucking in her blouse with her old dispatch.

But her dressier slacks present a different problem. A tighter fit, to be shapely, these slacks are difficult to pull over her hips. Left to her own efforts, she will pull them halfway, then wait for me to complete the job. She knows she looks good in these slacks, so she utters only mild protests as I wrench them up over her hips.

Recently we faced a major crisis. It began a few days after we sailed on a forty-day cruise of the Pacific. Suddenly, Jane forgot how to sit down—and, once down, forgot how to stand up. Nor could she remember how to lie down in bed.

Getting Jane to stand up became a nightmare. After a meal in the ship's dining room, with what felt like all eyes of the dining room focused on us, I'd try to get Jane to stand. But she would lean back and find an infinite number of ways to rearrange the flowers, the salt and pepper shakers, and the sugar bowl on the table. Eventually, I would think of something interesting or urgent to do and she'd quickly stand.

I've learned to be patient—and gentle. Above all, gentle.

I finally was able to show Jane how to hang on to the edge of the sink and slowly sit down on the toilet. The satisfaction in her eyes at this victory was worth all the trouble.

Jane cannot communicate coherently. As the weeks go by, she seems to understand less and less of what I say. Now, after some five years of illness, she talks mostly in unintelligible sounds. I try to sense what she thinks, what she wants and needs.

We try to walk at least one mile each day, in any kind of weather. She needs this exercise to maintain her healthy bone density—and to exercise her hip and leg muscles. Several years ago, when I left her out of my sight for a few moments, Jane fell from a low wall and broke off the ball of her right hip joint. It happened while we were visiting friends in Santa Barbara, California, where Cottage Hospital has some of the best orthopedic surgeons in the world. On the advice of an intern, I picked one surgeon who did a brilliant job of inserting a stainless steel ball-and-socket joint. Jane began to walk the next day.

Throughout her hospital stay, Jane's hip gave the staff less trouble than her Alzheimer's disease. At first, the head nurse banished me except for visiting hours. But the other nurses soon demanded that I be allowed to come in early and stay late. They wanted me to help feed Jane and assist in all the other care, including walking exercise.

Each Tuesday and Thursday Jane goes to a day-care center for Alzheimer's victims. As I get her ready to go, I talk to her about her friends at the center who love her and are waiting to see her. Her eyes light up with pleasure. She seems to anticipate the day ahead. During her first few days at the center, she would be tearful when I left her with the others. Within a week or so, though, she began waltzing off with the group as I left, not giving me a second thought.

I'm trying to help Jane experience some of the activities she has known before—and a few new ones. On our cruise, for example, I was pleased and proud of her as she slowly climbed the bus steps for our tours of such places as Tahiti, Auckland, Sydney, and Bali. She was afraid, at times, especially descending the bus steps. But she went on every shore excursion. And she seemed to enjoy these shore trips, although I'm sure she couldn't understand what she saw.

When I play golf, Jane rides with me in an electric cart. Near the greens, she'll climb down and watch us putt. Often she will applaud a good putt—even by my opponents.

A half dozen or so men members of our Springdale Golf Club make a special point of coming up to say hello to Jane and kiss her on the cheek. She beams at them.

Watching Jane enjoy beauty and babies makes taking care of her worth any trouble. She can say a few simple phrases quite clearly. She exclaims at a full moon over the South Pacific: "Isn't it beautiful?" When we shop at the supermarket, I make a special point of walking close to young mothers whose babies sit in their carts. Jane bends down to smile and croon to them. They always grin back at her. Surely, they understand each other.

How long can this last? I don't know. Nobody does. We're trying to flatten out the inevitable decline with the regimen of vitamins and minerals. As I've said, I'm sure they're helpful. Young nurses at Cottage Hospital gave me a chuckle. They expressed surprise and envy over Jane's youthful "skin tone." I naturally gave all the credit to vitamins and minerals, which was my way of tweaking ortho-dox medicine.

But the progressive decline seems inevitable. Early in her illness Jane and I could dance. Through the years her ability to walk steadily declined. Now, Jane shuffles in our walks and I must hold on to her at every step. She's stooped and often trembles.

Jane has almost forgotten how to feed herself. Some-times she can't seem to swallow. I feed her and help her drink.

Increasingly Jane talks in an unintelligible babble, although she can say "Good morning," and "Hello" and "Good-bye." There is one phrase she says very well, very well indeed, and does so vigorously and often to me: "I love you."

In some ways, caring for Jane is like having a three-year-old daughter. Although we never had a daughter, we have six granddaughters and one grandson. They live in vari-ous parts of the West, so we seldom see them except at reunions. Jane has never known the joy of baby-sitting for a grandchild.

Our sons, Alan and Guy and Paul, dearly love their mother. They call every week, at least, and talk to her on the telephone. Early in her illness, Jane could respond to their questions. She could ask questions of her own. And she could laugh at their stories of the little babies in their houses. As I watched her talk, I could see her love for them shining in her eyes and in her smile.

As time has gone on, however, Jane talks less and less—but she listens avidly. By the changes in her expression I can tell that she understands what they say. She smiles and nods her head. At the end of their conversation she can say "I love you" and "Good-bye."

Each of the sons has his own family, his own home, his own work to do. They can't fly into Princeton to be with us and visit Jane nearly as often as they'd like. Still, they can make it, even for a quick weekend, three or four times a year. Alan, living in St. Louis with wife Marilynne and two daughters, Karen and Claire, represents book publishing companies throughout the Midwest. Guy, who for some years was advertising acceptance manager for *Modern Maturity*, and later an executive with the Better Business Bureau of Los Angeles, lives with his wife, Linda, and daughter Lisa and son Dan, in LaCrescenta, a suburb of Los Angeles, and now teaches history in a private girls' high school. Paul, an auditor for the largest bank in Oregon, lives with his wife, Marcia, and their daughters, Jenny and Kate, and baby Emily, in Beaverton, a suburb of Portland.

Each of them suffers the sadness in his own way, crying privately over the loss of his mother. When we're together with Jane, we're so busy walking her, or feeding her, or taking her for a ride we have no time to cry. But in private moments with Jane, I've seen Paul sitting holding her closely and kissing her cheek. Alan, too, likes to sit facing her, holding her hands, talking earnestly to her about his love, how the kids are doing. Guy has been in a position to help me handle Jane's wheelchair on our trips to the West Coast and the busy-ness helps him cope with his grief. He gives Jane big hugs and kisses. And Jane responds to each of them with smiles and kisses.

If Jane were alone and ill, I know each of the sons would move heaven and earth to care for her as well as possible. I think they believe I am taking care of her about as well as could be expected. This surely is a relief to them, as is the knowledge that we have the funds to provide for her care.

They're concerned about me, too. Without expressing their concerns in so many words, they want me to stay well. They love me and feel I am important to them. So they inquire about how I'm feeling, what I'm doing, how my golf game is. They like nothing better than to tease me, saying I'm always complaining about my game—but somehow always come up with good scores and continue to beat them. They want to know what I'm thinking and when I'll come to visit them.

While I wish we could all be together, to talk and dream and argue over baseball teams, basketball, and football, we can't. But we do the best we can. And it's important to know that, as always, we all love each other.

As I watch Jane decline, I experience a shock at every change. Even though I know each change is coming, I'm never emotionally prepared. Always it seems so sad I cannot bear it. But at that point, I'll notice that Jane needs a diaper changed, or could eat a cookie and drink a glass of juice. Or it's time for a walk. And then I'm too busy to think about being sad.

Someday, it will all be over and Jane will be at peace. Thankfully, she has never known what has happened to her. There is no pain. She may—or may not—go before I pass on. I'm trying to take care of myself carefully, for her sake as well as mine. It's not likely, but she could linger for some years yet. In any case, I'll try to go on doing the things Jane would want me to do: enjoy our children and grandchildren, and our home . . . travel . . . shoot more pars and birdies . . . write. . . .

At the moment, though, we have an important, immediate objective. I'm trying to teach Jane to let me wash her ears.

5

Our Next Step: Praxilene

My heart started pounding in mounting excitement the day I saw the news item.

Our dear friend, Harold Baron, clipped a small story he had seen in a Long Island paper. The news story came from Albert Einstein College of Medicine in the Bronx. There, the Department of Gerontology was seeking victims of Alzheimer's who might wish to participate in a new experimental research project.

If she were able, I knew, Jane would eagerly volunteer for such an experiment. So I immediately called the telephone number and talked to a Dr. Miriam Aronson. She sounded vigorous, forthright, and encouraging. Perhaps, I thought—I hoped—we were on the verge of a cure!

Over the phone I told her everything I knew about Jane and her diagnoses. It must have been adequate, for she encouraged me to bring Jane to their offices for an interview. It was 1981, a year after Jane was diagnosed as being ill.

I've always been proud of Jane, but I was especially proud

of her that morning. She carried herself with eager poise, smiling, saying cheery hellos to everyone. She showed a willingness, even an eagerness, to talk with the neurologists and medical people who put her through the tests.

Jane began a battery of oral tests of cognitive comprehension. In her lifetime, she had taken many tests, triumphing in all of them. So she almost eagerly submitted to these new ones.

Jane was able to answer perhaps half of the questions accurately. As I watched the faces of those who gave her the tests I could see veiled concern. But I said nothing and waited.

The experiment, I discovered, involved a European drug called Praxilene. It could not be sold in this country but was already being widely used in western Europe. In general terms, the neurologists explained to me, the drug enhanced blood supply to the brain. Perhaps, they thought, this could have some positive effect on the progress of the disease. It seemed reasonable to me.

Once a week, Jane and I would leave the house in Princeton before 6 A.M., always dark during the winter months, for the sixty-plus-mile drive to the Bronx. There were the usual traffic tie-ups along the way and at George Washington Bridge. The morning trip across the Cross Bronx Expressway was always hair-raising, dodging in and out between the trucks, keeping an eye out for the northbound Bronx River Parkway.

After several trips, I was pleased to see, Jane seemed to know the way. She could speak a few phrases.

"We turn right," she would say.

"That's right, darling," I'd say. "Thank you for helping me. You just keep on helping me that way."

I could see by the calm sense of satisfaction on her face that Jane felt, in the nicest sense, that she had helped me. This was long after she was unable to say anything but the simplest of phrases.

Albert Einstein College of Medicine, located across the

street from the Bronx Community Hospital, presented a real parking problem. We soon began planning for enough time to park five or six blocks away. Then we would walk from our car to the hospital, glad at least that it would help us get in our walking for the day.

Each visit required an analysis of blood and urine, along with a blood-pressure test. Then a staff neurologist would talk with Jane and ask her to walk for him, testing her coordination and steadiness.

Again, I was so proud of this plucky girl. More and more Jane seemed to be a dear little daughter to me. Jane's youthful looks, her general health, and her ability to walk, nonplussed the neurologists.

Each week, the staff would ask me if I saw any change in Jane. Desperately I wanted to be able to say, "Yes, she's improving." But I couldn't.

Each time I seemed to disappoint them, for I could not report either any improvement or any obvious decline. Jane seemed much the same, week to week. If anything, as the year passed, she was talking less and walking with somewhat shorter steps.

During that year, Jane began to be incontinent. Again, it was a shock to me, for it was a major indication of the disease's effect. Learning how to prepare for this, and handle it without upsetting Jane, was a job in itself. There's nothing special about coping with incontinence, of course. I bought the special diapers—I preferred Attends—and tried to time the periods of urination. Perhaps half the time we'd get to the toilet before Jane urinated.

As so often happened in changes of this sort, my heart would ache for Jane. She knew she didn't want to urinate into her pad or her pants. But she couldn't tell me she needed to go to the toilet. At the last moment, when she suddenly felt the urge to go, she would clutch her groin and call out "Oh! Oh!" I'd simply hold her and soothe her and say "It's all right, sweetheart. It's all right. We'll just take care of it." And she would sigh.

Each week, in the tests of cognitive comprehension, Jane was doing less well. After the first seven months, the staff gave me a worried report.

"Jane didn't answer a single question correctly this morning."

"I'm sorry," I said. There was nothing I could do except ache—and ache for Jane.

At the end of a year, I was given the bad news.

"We're stopping the program," Dr. Aronson told me. "We don't have enough definitive data to report. There isn't enough for the Food and Drug Administration to make a decision. And the company has decided not to fund any more experiments. We're sorry."

Once again I was disappointed, sad—and discouraged.

"If you feel there were any benefits at all to Jane," Dr. Aronson went on, "you can order the drug directly from Belgium and continue giving it to her. Or you can get it in Canada."

I thanked the staff and Dr. Aronson. Dr. Robert Katzman, the head of the research into Alzheimer's and of the work of the gerontology department, had interviewed Jane and me during the project. He was quiet and encouraging, urging us to keep on doing what we could to stay as healthy as possible.

We arranged for Jane to be under the continuing care of Dr. Leon Thal, a tall, slender, youthful-looking neurologist with an eager manner who seemed to care about his patients. We began to see him every two months. To Jane, he was kind and thoughtful, helping her in every way. To me, he was direct and candid.

"Mr. Wirsig," he said, "in early-onset cases of this kind, the average life span from time of diagnosis is seven years. Some lives are shorter, a few longer. But that's the average. Jane seems in remarkably good shape. She still walks well. And she's responsive."

"I may be feeding her too much, doctor," I said, worrying as usual. "She now weighs 136 pounds. That's about ten pounds more than she's ever weighed before."

"That's all right," Dr. Thal said. "Try not to go above 136. But keep up the feeding as long as she eats well. The time will come soon enough when—when we'll face the opposite problem."

Again, I felt a chill of dread at what must be in store for Jane.

We said good-bye to the staff and doctors, all of whom had come to be good friends.

"Come see us," they said. "And if we come across anything else that has any chance of helping Jane, we'll call you."

Each staff member gave Jane a kiss. She beamed at them with her lovely smile, her blue eyes glistening.

To show how willingly Jane entered such experimental programs, and why she seemed so "special" to all who knew her, I'll describe as much of her life and background as I know.

A lovely style of grace, of quietly always doing her best, characterized Jane's life almost from its beginning. She was born in Brookline, Massachusetts, into an Irish family that was devoutly Catholic. Their parish priest was Bishop Spellman, long before he became a controversial cardinal in New York. Jane's father, a successful candy salesman, identified with Boston College and became a big fan of its sports programs, supporting the college more passionately than if he had been a graduate.

Jane's mother became increasingly difficult to live with. She was a constant complainer who never—never—forgave anyone any slight. And never forgave her husband anything.

Still, Jane remembered many family pleasures, like the Sunday afternoon drives in their big sedan with her two sisters and two brothers. Each summer, for many years, they spent vacations in Hyannis Port on Cape Cod.

Steadily, without flamboyance, Jane excelled in everything she tried in high school. An honors student, she worked on her high school newspaper and was editor of her high school yearbook. Like many of her classmates, she got a crush on her mathematics teacher. She loved to root for her high school football team.

Jane had one boyfriend who was more special to her than others. For many years after we were married she exchanged Christmas cards with him.

By the time Jane was ready for college, her mother and father were living apart. Lack of any extra family money meant that, despite some scholarship funds which she was awarded, Jane had to work during the school year. During summer vacations, she worked as a waitress in Cape Cod restaurants.

Jane had a gift—a gift she possessed all her life—of being beloved by almost all who knew her. This quality was especially evident during her college career at Vassar and in graduate school.

A classmate of Jane's at Vassar, who had attended excellent private schools before going to college, tells how Jane developed.

"When we were freshmen," she says, "I was what you'd call 'ahead' of Jane simply because a private school gave us more of the college techniques than a public school would. But Jane applied herself. It wasn't long at all before Jane caught up to me. And then, being a brilliant person, she soon passed me in every academic way."

Jane's brilliance in the academic world, instead of creating envy, endeared her to her classmates. They seemed proud of her and took special joy in her accomplishments.

At Vassar, Jane was neither a "drone" nor an active dater. She simply had to work and study in much of her spare time. A careless boy, looking at Jane at the time, might not think of her as beautiful. Yet she wanted to be desirable to boys and always dressed as attractively as she could. She gave special care to her hair and nails. With a smile, she would speak of her legs as "my one asset."

What Jane didn't realize, of course, was that her slender figure--she often called herself "too skinny"—was quite soft and rounded. She never thought of her breasts as a sexual ornament, yet they were full and the right size for her figure.

Above all, Jane had beautiful eyes. Light blue, they always seemed to shine with good humor and love.

No one boyfriend seemed to emerge in college, although friends arranged double dates. She remembered with some amusement a blind date she once had with Elliott Richardson, a friend of a classmate's Harvard boyfriend, who has since become an eminent lawyer and world-famous advisor to presidents.

"He was drunk the entire time," she said, humor combined with disgust in her voice.

One of Jane's biggest crises at Vassar was the swimming test required of every graduating student. With a thrashing dog paddle, Jane could swim a short distance. But she could never dive headfirst into the water. The requirement stipulated that a student must dive into the water and swim twenty-five feet.

Again and again Jane tried to meet the requirement, failing always in her willingness to dive into the pool headfirst. Finally, the instructor "averted" her gaze while Jane slid into the water at the side of the pool and paddled her required twenty-five feet.

With a sigh of relief, Jane "passed" in swimming, probably the only average score she ever received in her life.

In her junior year, Jane was elected to Phi Beta Kappa. She was editor of her Vassar yearbook. And when she was graduated, Vassar awarded her a rare fellowship to the Graduate School of Journalism at Columbia University in New York—a fellowship that would pay tuition, board, and room.

That summer, between graduation from Vassar and entering Columbia, Jane and two classmates, Pat Burdine and Jane O'Connor, published an advocacy newspaper in Poughkeepsie. The paper, and the girls' living expenses, were supported by Pat Burdine, heiress of the Burdine family department store in Miami. The excitement and discipline of putting out that paper was a milestone in Jane's growth. Later, she often reflected with pleasure and some awe on what these slips of girls tried—and succeeded—in doing.

I'll always remember my first glimpse of Jane at journalism school. I'd come across country from Los Angeles by bus, the main part of my luggage being an old L. C. Smith manual typewriter. I was already set up in the large "newsroom" of the school, my typewriter installed, when I saw her enter.

Dressed in a pink plaid suit, Jane was lugging her portable typewriter. Right away I noticed her slender figure, her nice long legs, her graceful walk. She had a glow in her eyes and a smile for everyone. Her golden hair, loose and graceful, fell to her shoulders. Above all, I noticed her beautiful eyes were somehow soft yet laughing. She chose a desk in the row right behind me.

From the beginning, Jane's writing and thinking abilities made her stand out from all the other students. The professors immediately recognized her talents. And she accepted their attention quietly, modestly, and buried herself in the work and in getting to know her classmates.

Later, Jane said she was attracted to me immediately. It was so, I suppose, for I never knew her to dissemble. But like an oaf, I ignored her most of that whole first semester. True, I had to work. Nights, for my board, I waited on tables in the college after-hours Lion's Den. On weekends, I wrote news shows for radio station WQXR.

All journalism students aimed for the mid-term prizes in the "law of libel," a class offered that first term. The prize paid the second semester's tuition.

Jane, of course, won that prize. I did manage to win a lesser prize—the job of secretary to the Pulitzer Prize Committee of Judges that year. And that paid my second term tuition.

The job was tedious, involving classifying and cataloging entries. My one memorable contribution, as I remember it, was to retrieve a big roll of newspapers tossed on the floor and about to be thrown out. These papers had been sent from Manila without explanation or covering letter. I opened the papers, glanced over them, and noticed they carried a series by one Carlos Romulo who, if my memory isn't too bad, was editor of the paper.

What could I lose? I entered this series, filled out an entry blank, classified, and cataloged it. Of course—it won a major Pulitzer Prize.

Jane said, later, that she was waiting for me to come to my senses about her. Not until our second semester was I even the least bit wise enough to pay special attention to her. Our classmates included Maggie Higgins, a flighty blonde from California who spent a lot of time talking to the men students, and Flora Lewis, also from California, who had a voluptuous figure, knew it, and therefore moved languorously at half-speed all of the time.

When I volunteered to head up one of the teams in the radio writing classes taught by CBS's Paul White, Jane, I noticed, decided to be on my team. I also noticed that she happened to be in the newsroom, working on her assignments, when I was there.

We began talking about our work, our assignments. We began to eat lunch together. We talked and talked—endlessly talked—about our professors, about careers, about radio writing . . . and about ourselves. Jane's grace, and straightforward thinking, were never more evident than when I told her I was married. She winced. But that didn't stop her from our lunches and talks together.

Jane began to visit me while I worked in the Lion's Den, sitting in a corner to study while I waited on tables. The jukebox held all the current big band numbers. Our favorite—and it has remained our favorite for forty-eight years—was Glenn Miller's rollicking "Chattanooga Choo Choo." Whenever business was slack, I'd plug in a dime and we'd enjoy swinging to "Chattanooga Choo Choo" on the Lion's Den dance floor.

To be sure, I was regarded as a somewhat better-than-average dancer at Kearney State Teachers College. Smooth. Jane's natural grace and eagerness enabled her to follow me precisely. We were good together. Jane knew it better than I.

Just when Jane began to love me she never said, exactly. Like the slow dolt that I was, I didn't realize until the second semester was under way that she was a girl I simply could not live the rest of my life without.

Then my main concern inevitably became, Would Jane love me? I was trying hard in classes but the professors regarded me as a rebel, a maverick. One day, for example, when the New York *Times* managing editor, Bob Garst, was critiquing the "front page" my group had put together, he looked at the eight-column, 72-point screaming headline I'd written, imitating the Los Angeles *Times*, and dismissed it with a wave of his hand. "Well," he said in disgust, "the New York *Times* would *never* do anything like that."

Jane, however, was a rising star to everyone. Her ability and perceptions promised a great future. She towered over Maggie Higgins and Flora Lewis. And I'm sure she would have continued to tower over them if she had remained in the news business.

So I wondered how this star-in-the-making could possibly be really interested in me. At the time, a weekly salary of fifty dollars sounded like the pinnacle achievement of a lifetime. I wondered if I could ever make it.

Gently, with quiet grace and dignity, Jane made herself available to my schedule. There were times, after class, when Jane, Maggie Higgins, and I would have a beer—

Dutch treat. Higgins rebelled at Dutch, thinking of herself as a pretty young thing who was entitled to be treated by men. But Jane, hating every swallow of beer, but drinking it gamely to be with me, was willing to pay for her own.

Our talks usually ranged over a wide spectrum. When I learned Jane was Catholic, I naturally had to unburden myself to her about my vigorous dislike of the temporal church, and my lack of belief in God or an afterlife.

Quietly, her tone so different from my excited emphasis, Jane explained that she, too, had split with her Church on an intellectual basis. Indeed, her senior thesis had been a logical discussion of the reasoning that convinced her to leave the Church. My admiration for her rose many notches higher.

In fact, I found myself with all the feelings of love. I enjoyed the beauty of her eyes, her hair, and, despite the slight stoop in her shoulders from studying and writing so much, her lovely figure.

Slowly, without any noticeable "moment," we began talking about loving each other. At the same time, because of my marriage, we couldn't talk of future "plans," so we didn't try. Both of us, I think, were marking time, playing it by ear.

As usual, I was thinking ahead about the kind of writing that seemed most exciting and valuable to me. During my spare time at school, and at WQXR, I worked on magazine articles. To me, the ultimate success would be writing articles for the *Saturday Evening Post, Collier's, Esquire, Reader's Digest, Coronet, Look.* These were the big, major media of the time.

So as usual, on Sunday afternoon, December 7, 1941, I was on duty at WQXR and had an article in my typewriter. The persistent ringing of the bulletin bell on the teletypes kept annoying me. Finally, muttering to myself, I got up and hurried over to see what caused the commotion. The first bulletin came from the White House, announcing that the Japanese had attacked Pearl Harbor.

I guess I was moving swiftly. I edited the teletype and took it into the radio announcer's booth. The announcer immediately cut into whatever symphony was on and made the announcement—beating CBS, NBC, and ABC.

War, I realized, was closer to me than I ever thought it would be. I had registered for the draft in California. While at Occidental College, in Los Angeles, I'd tried to enter the Navy's officer training program. I sought a commission on the basis of my college work in journalism. But I wasn't accepted—and I wasn't surprised. Radical activities and editorials in school were already following me. So I'd gone off to journalism school.

Now the war added to our anxiety. We were in love. But it was the imminence of graduation, the possibility of going off in different directions, perhaps of losing Jane forever, that finally thrust me into a discussion with Jane. What would we do?

She told me she loved me—and I could hardly believe it. I hadn't won any of the year-end prizes and was questioning, basically, my ability and competence. Jane, on the other hand, had won one of the three prized Pulitzer Traveling Fellowships that would pay $1,500—a fortune, then—for a year's living and travel in a foreign country. Jane took me by the hand, reassuring me that whatever happened she would stay with me.

We both decided to apply for jobs at CBS radio. Jane immediately got a job in the main newsroom of the CBS radio network—and within days was writing the biggest news program of the day, the "Morning News Roundup." She would call in Edward R. Murrow, William Shirer, Charles Collingwood, and others from around the world, knitting their reports together with her brilliant narrative. At twenty-two, just out of journalism school, this girl was writing professional news shows.

I, on the other hand, got a job on the lobster shift—from midnight to 8:30 A.M.—at CBS shortwave, across the street from Jane's newsroom.

To live, we found rooms in a bug-infested rooming house near International House because the price fit our salaries, which were $35 per week. We could catch the double-decker Fifth Avenue buses to and from work—Jane in the daytime, me at night.

I asked my wife for a divorce, suggesting she get it in Mexico, and said that I would pay for it. She was angry and hurt, but she went ahead and got the divorce. My mother, thinking that I'd been trapped by some opportunistic woman who had designs on my future, which, like all mothers, she felt would be significant, set out by bus to New York to save me from myself. She arrived, then decided she'd like to meet Jane at breakfast before work. I'd given Jane my Phi Gamma Delta pin as a symbol of our engagement, since I didn't have the money for a ring. When Jane entered the restaurant and caught sight of my mother, not realizing she would see my mother so soon that morning, she frantically removed the pin, not wanting to offend my mother in any way.

How it all went is hazy to me. It seemed to me that in a few minutes my mother recognized all the values I saw in Jane and was won over. I was glad, for I'd have married Jane over anyone's objections.

Next, I began to fight my draft board, claiming my work at CBS shortwave, in which I did some propaganda analysis, was vital to the war effort. The head of my draft board, the controller of Occidental College, whose older son had entered the Air Force and would soon be piloting bombers over Europe, could not get excited over my claims of doing propaganda analysis for "our side." What he remembered, of course, were editorials in the Occidental college paper, signed by me but written by my radical friends Rod Voigt and George Hatch, who enjoyed pouring out their wrath at the government over my name. At the time, I couldn't have cared less; I even professed to believe what they were writing. Actually, I was so busy working nights at Lockheed and weekends at the Sears credit department, taking sixteen hours of credits, and running the Occidental News Service that I had no time to be concerned about words they put in my mouth.

After an acerbic exchange of letters, I demanded to have my induction procedure take place in New York. I felt, then, that I would not be included into the Army for perhaps six or eight months.

With that amount of time ahead of us, Jane and I decided to get married. We had to do it over a weekend if we were not to miss work and keep to our schedules. My immediate boss was Hubert Pryor. Years later, in a bemused fashion, he asked why I hadn't requested time off to get married and honeymoon. But the thought hadn't occurred to us; in retrospect, it would have been nice, of course.

We couldn't be married in New York, because of blood test requirements and those time factors, so we arranged to be married by the Reverend Bliss in a Congregational church in Greenwich. To our delight, Jane O'Connor and Pat Burdine agreed to be our witnesses, the four of us riding up to Greenwich on the train. Reverend Bliss didn't mind that I had been divorced; he was more interested in whether we loved each other.

That began the happiest period of my life, which happened to be the rest of my life, and lasted from 1942 until the present. Jane made me happy with her steadfast love, her support, and all the ways in which she was a wonderful wife, mother, lover, and companion.

Several months after taking a little apartment on Perry Street, on the edge of the Village, I learned that I would be inducted.

"Let's take a honeymoon trip to Mexico City," I suggested. "We'll scout the place for your year's Pulitzer trip. You can't go anywhere else until the war's over. And who knows when that will be."

By this time Jane knew she was pregnant, which suffused her with a wondering kind of happiness. She would walk along Fifth Avenue, looking at herself in the shop windows, thinking about the changes that would come over her in a few months. I began to call her by a name that became her favorite. From then on, in fun and loving moments, she became my "gammy mammy."

To anyone else, perhaps, it would seem silly to travel cross-country by train, then from El Paso down to Mexico City by train, for only a three-day weekend, then return to Los Angeles. There I would leave Jane, at my mother's, while I returned to New York for induction.

Like any other tourists, we crowded as much as we could into our days and nights. We enjoyed lunching and snacking at Sanborn's. We sailed through the floating gardens at Xochamilco, walked in Chapultepec Park, wandered around the Palacio of Belles Arts and the Zocalo, looking through the gates at government buildings closed for the weekend. We returned to Los Angeles happy, pleased with our trip and liking what we saw in Mexico City. Jane decided that was where she'd take her Pulitzer Prize traveling fellowship trip.

Both of us cried when I said good bye, leaving on a train for New York to be inducted. Neither of us knew what was in store for us. But we were glad that we were having a baby in case I never came back.

Thousands of GIs will remember the Grand Central Annex. I went through that big, noisy mill of induction. The day was cold, the Annex impersonal. So much of that day I sat naked and vulnerable.

Finally, with a casual motion and offhand remarks I can still see and hear, a medic handed me my papers. *Rejected.* Sudden relief mingled with apprehension. I wondered if a mistake had been made. I asked to talk to one of the doctors involved in my examination. One of them did take a few moments to talk with me.

"Did you ever have tuberculosis?" he asked.

"Never," I said.

"Well, you did once," he said. "You have a big calcified node on your lungs. It's bigger than the Army allows. We couldn't afford the risk of having you break it and come down with tuberculosis—and support you for the rest of your life. I suggest you see your doctor when you get home."

I was frightened. But the fright was tempered with relief that I would not be going into the Army. Later, I figured that the men who had been inducted with me were caught in the Battle of the Bulge. But for my calcified node, I probably would have faced the German blitz in that attack. The rest of my life, I figured, would be on borrowed time.

As quickly as I could I called Jane, telling her I had been rejected and was coming home.

"We'll be together," I yelled, crying a little.

"It's wonderful. It's wonderful," she was saying, over and over again. And she, too, was crying a little.

Then I visited a doctor whom we knew in New York. I kept trying to think of when I might have been actively tubercular. Probably, I decided, it was during my last year in Occidental, when I was working a full eight-hour shift at night at Lockheed, taking sixteen hours of studies, running the Occidental News Bureau—and not getting much sleep.

The doctor X-rayed me, then talked reassuringly to me.

"Everybody has calcified nodes on their lungs," he said. "Everybody at one time or another has a mild case of tuberculosis. The body fights it. The lungs wall off the tubercular nodes with calcium.

"Your node," he went on, "is slightly larger than Army regulations allow. But—you'll probably live a normal, long, and healthy life."

Jane and I took about five seconds to decide that I'd go with her on her Pulitzer fellowship trip. Soon we were heading back to Mexico by train. A Mexican friend, Ernesto Aviles Valles, whom we had met on our first trip, put us in touch with a señora who ran a boardinghouse for Mexican college students. She provided us with a large bedroom-sitting room and bath, and board, for a price we could afford.

We had about three months, we figured. Then we'd have to head back to the States for our baby to be born. That meant Jane's year-long fellowship would have to be shortened by nine months. But with a war on, we were lucky to have any time at all.

Since Mexico City was high, more than a mile above sea level, we knew malaria-carrying mosquitoes wouldn't bother Jane. We decided there was enough to do, to see, and to study in Mexico City itself. No side trips to lower altitudes for us!

Jane went through those months looking lovelier and, to be sure, more motherly, every day. I busied myself with three magazine articles I wanted to write and sell.

American magazines, I figured, should be interested in the Mexican comedian Cantinflas, Sanborn's restaurant and silver business, and Mexico's foreign minister Ezequiel Padilla. I expected some success because Jane and I had already sold our first magazine article.

During my overnight stints at CBS shortwave, I had begun collecting anecdotes about pets in the armed services that came over the teletypes during dull periods of the night. After collecting dozens of such stories, I put together a draft of an article called "Pets in the Armed Forces." Then Jane took my draft and wrote a draft. Then I wrote another draft. We soon realized that each of us contributed different things to the finished article, both of which were needed. I had a good sense of structure. I could write dialogue and build anecdotes with beginnings, middles, and punch-line endings. Jane, on the other hand, provided her flawlessly smooth narrative style.

Together we produced an article that we sent to a young literary agent we'd met in New York, Ann Elmo. Within a week she had sold it to the *Saturday Evening Post* for $500. It wasn't the great sum they gave to major writers, but it was our first sale—and we'd have been happy with $50.

When the article appeared some months later, we learned that the *Post* had sent its famous photographer Ivan Dmitri around the world to photograph mascots in the armed forces—in color—especially for our article. The *Post* editors opened the article with a handsome, four-color spread. They also printed a biographical sketch of Jane and me, along with the photograph we'd had taken soon after our wedding. In that picture, Jane looked appropriately glamorous and I, of course, looked like a wimp.

As everyone knows, success stimulates. Once the *Post* had taken our first article, I wrote a piece on Paul White, the talented news executive at CBS News who had put together the team of Ed Murrow, Shirer, Collingwood, and others. The article featured the humor and anger I felt when my boss switched me to the day-side at shortwave news to be with Jane—and Paul White immediately switched Jane to the night schedule. The article promptly sold to *Esquire*.

Then I got to work on a profile of Edward R. Murrow, then in London. I researched what I could in the files. I interviewed his associates at CBS in New York. I wrote the article on a portable typewriter while riding the chair car returning to Los Angeles after my rejection by the Army. I'm sure I drove other passengers mad with my constant tapping, yet none of them complained. By the end of the three-day trip I had finished the article. It sold immediately to *Coronet*—the first profile of Murrow, whose name became synonymous with quality for TV network news.

With those articles finished, I felt confident that success would continue with the articles from Mexico. I didn't bother to query magazine editors in advance. I had no "name," so editors wouldn't be likely to give me an assignment. I simply picked out subjects I thought had a good chance of selling and plunged ahead.

I was sure that Cantinflas, Sanborn's, and Padilla would make good subjects for magazines. And, indeed, they were successful—all going to *Coronet*. As it turned out,

Jane preferred to spend her time writing reports on what she saw, what she heard, what she thought about Mexico. These reports were to fulfill her requirement for the Pulitzer traveling fellowship.

Friends have often told me that the dean of the journalism school, Carl W. Ackerman, never forgave me for marrying Jane and "taking her away from a great career in journalism." It was undoubtedly true. As I've said, Jane towered over Marguerite Higgins, who later became a notorious war correspondent, and Flora Lewis, now a pundit for the New York *Times.* In my opinion, and many others', I might add, Jane would have far surpassed their later accomplishments if she had continued, alone and unencumbered, in reporting and writing.

The dean's attitude didn't make me mad. I agreed. Later, though, I had to laugh with some irony. After I had become editor-in-chief of *Look* and *Woman's Home Companion* magazines, he would sometimes remark to his associates how I was "one of his favorite pupils" in journalism school and that he always "knew I would go far."

Jane chose marriage to me, and having children, instead of a formal career—sensing, perhaps, that eventually she could have a career, too. We returned from Mexico in late summer 1943, and our first son, Alan, was born in November.

As anyone who knows her would understand, Jane became a remarkable young mother. Somehow, instinctively, she understood time and motion management. Almost effortlessly, she combined feeding, toileting, clothing, walking, housekeeping, shopping, and house accounting, all without a flap. Loving and kind to begin with, she brought her intelligence to bear on rearing our sons, Alan, Guy, and Paul.

With delightful élan, she also began to learn to cook. "I'm learning to cook like my mother did," she said, smiling. "I liked her cooking. And I'm beginning to like my cooking."

Jane could make a mistake, though, and when she did, as Fiorello La Guardia used to say, it was a "beaut." In mixing the baby formula for our first son, Alan, Jane misunderstood the directions and prepared it with one-and-a half times the appropriate amount. As the weeks went on, our Alan became a little tub of fat. He was cute and healthy, but a fat baby. We couldn't figure it out. Then Jane, in reviewing her procedures, discovered herself what she had been doing wrong. Back on the proper formula, Alan soon lost his excess fat and began a sturdy growth into a healthy little boy.

We often talked about her writing skills. She must not lose them, we agreed. I was pleased that she wanted to continue with some form of writing. So I encouraged her, while kept at home with the babies, to try some short fiction.

Sure enough, Jane's first short story was about a baby. And our agent, Ann Elmo, promptly sold it to the Sunday magazine section of a Canadian newspaper. That was the only fiction Jane ever wrote.

Jane ghosted several books for Thomas Y. Crowell publishers. One of them, a book telling the exploits of a Dutch underground worker during World War II, gave me some irritated moments. I met the man and immediately took a dislike to him—arrogant, a womanizer, I was sure. I didn't like the idea of Jane's traveling into New York to meet with him in his hotel room to get his story. As it turned out, she, too, thought he was a blowhard. She assured me she could handle any situation that might come up. She turned out a fine, professional job.

While I was away from home for a few months, taking a round-the-world trip for *Look* Magazine, Jane had an experience with her Aunt Nell that showed Jane's sense of humor even under trying circumstances. Jane's Aunt Nell, a spinster sister of her mother's, had worked all her life for AT&T and was now living in retirement in a hotel in New York. When Aunt Nell became eighty-eight years old, she reached the point where she could no longer handle her own affairs. She must have suffered psychological problems, too, for one day the hotel staff found her huddled in her closet.

Jane called Dr. Stone for help. He immediately went down to the hotel, took Aunt Nell out, and made arrangements to admit her to a rest home in Croton-on-Hudson. Jane asked her sister, Nancy, to stay with the boys and asked Nancy's new husband, Bob, to drive with her up to the Croton rest home with Aunt Nell.

"It was after dark before they got started," said Nancy. "But Aunt Nell happily put on her hat and gloves—a Boston lady *never* goes without her gloves!—and got into the car. Bob drove, Aunt Nell sat in the middle, and Jane was on the outside.

"All the way up the Hudson, Aunt Nell thought she was on her way to a 'restaurant' and eagerly awaited their arrival. Jane tried patiently to explain to her that it was a 'rest home' and, for a moment, Aunt Nell would accept that—and then talk about what she was going to have for dinner.

"She kept turning to Bob and asking him, 'Dr. Stone, did anyone ever tell you how much you look like my Nancy's Bob?'

"The trip seemed to take forever and was exhausting to Jane and to Bob. But Aunt Nell was happy, looking forward to a drink and dinner.

"On arrival at the rest home, the three went into the waiting area and sat down side by side, with Aunt Nell in the middle. A nurse came to greet them. She looked at Bob, bleary-eyed from a long day's work and a long drive after dark on unfamiliar roads. She looked at Jane, also slightly bleary-eyed after her long day and worried about her beloved Aunt Nell. And she looked at Aunt Nell, bright-eyed and eager to get on to the next step, going in to dinner.

"'Which one,' the nurse asked, 'is the patient?;

"Jane looked across Aunt Nell to where Bob was seated and pointed to him. Not to be outdone, Bob pointed to Jane. All the while Aunt Nell just smiled."

Nancy remembers how Jane, at a crucial time in her life, was helpful to her. "When Mother and Daddy separated, and we left the big house in West Newton, Mother, little brother Bobby, and I moved into a rooming house and ate all of our meals in the local greasy spoon, or out of cans heated on a hot plate.

"After I was graduated from high school, I worked for a while in Boston, and had a lot of personal problems. Then Jane took me under her wing, offering to let me come and live with her. I was scared to death. I had no idea what I could do to earn a living, had never been around little babies for a long period of time, and had not lived in a 'normal' home for many years.

"The very first day I was in Jane's home she made me feel important. I think she purposely gave me tasks to do for baby Guy so that I could feel his little warm arms around my neck and make me feel loved and needed.

"At the time, Jane was only twenty-seven years old herself. She was the mother of two little boys, a loving and caring wife to her husband—and the best role model I could have ever had."

From time to time, I'd ask Jane if she wanted to write or rewrite materials for the magazines I edited. She was always glad to do it, and always turned out excellent work.

During the years I was editor of *Woman's Home Companion*, I had our good friend, Margaret Thompson Biddle, report regularly from Paris on interesting people she met and events she attended. Margaret, gracious and beautiful, was one of the world's wealthiest women and moved in any circle she liked. Often this meant lunching with her friends Wallis Simpson and the Duke of Windsor as well as Edward R. Murrow and other American correspondents.

No dilettante, Margaret Biddle worked at her job. Knowing, or at least accepting, the fact that she could not write appropriately for a regular column, she didn't mind that I turned her work over to Jane for rewriting. The two worked together to produce a light, gossipy column often filled with real meat. They could handle important events well, letting our readers experience a world they'd otherwise never know.

Our sons were growing and doing well in school. A housekeeper came in every day to cook and take care of the house. It seemed natural enough for Jane to go back to work. She eased into it by participating with me in a little public relations company we formed with two friends, Tom O'Connor and Dave Gordon, both formerly of *Look* magazine. Among other clients, we took on consulting work for Opinion Research Corporation and Gallup and Robinson, two research organizations that Gallup had helped found years before in Princeton.

At once Jane became a favorite with both organizations, trusted completely and admired for calm, steady production and advice. She was superb.

News of her work got around to Educational Testing Service. Jack Rimalover, then the publicity and public relations executive for ETS, persuaded Jane and me to come talk with ETS president Henry Chauncey. The purpose: to be considered as public relations consultants for ETS.

Chauncey liked Jane at once. We both liked him very much. The arrangement was made. Jane immediately started going into an office at ETS and working regular hours.

Of all the examples of Jane's ability, one of the best is the story of her first annual report. Chauncey, having great plans for the growth of ETS, had also brought on board a well-known, high-powered public relations consulting team from Earl Newsome and Company in New York. Arthur Tourtellot, one member of the team, was a scholar, a historian, as well as experienced advisory executive at

Columbia Broadcasting System. He also had a Harvard accent and a suave, authoritative manner some people found impressive. Along with Tourtellot came the Newsome executive vice president.

Our first meeting with Tourtellot and his associate came after they had been consulting for some months. Executives at ETS had already chosen sides: Some liked the public relations men, others thought them pompous and ignorant of educational matters. For their first project, they turned out a draft of Henry Chauncey's "message" for the ETS annual report. It was typical of annual report messages they wrote for other corporations: general, sweeping, inexact, lacking both an understanding of ETS and its future, and the specifics that Henry Chauncey wanted to get across.

The discussion was calm and civil. The public relations men repeated that they felt an annual report should be just what they had produced—something that wouldn't tell too much, would read smoothly, and would set the stage for the facts and figures in the rest of the annual report.

Henry, not knowing exactly how to carry on the discussion about what he wanted but found difficult to describe, kept raising questions about the Tourtellot version. I interjected several of my own caustic comments, the kind that always seem to generate more heat than light.

Finally, about the time everyone reached the point of exasperation and exhaustion, Jane calmly said: "Let me take it over the weekend and see what we might do." She had by now worked long enough with Henry Chauncey to sense what he was finding difficult to say, both in conversation and on paper. Besides, Jane had been intensively learning what ETS was all about.

The public relations men nodded sagely to each other and then murmured how good an idea they thought it was—and left.

Working all weekend was nothing new for Jane. In college, and at journalism school, and while we were writing our articles, working at the typewriter on Saturday and Sunday was no big deal.

Jane wrote a draft of an annual report that Saturday and Sunday. Early Monday morning, she turned in the draft to Henry Chauncey. He was delighted with it and promptly had copies mailed to Tourtellot and his associate. In a few days, telephone word came to Chauncey from the Newsome office: Both public relations men liked and admired Jane's draft very, very much.

Their admiration for Jane increased manyfold. From then on, they regarded Jane with great confidence and trust.

For the next ten years or so, Jane wrote Henry Chauncey's message for the ETS annual report. Lest anyone think these were casual pieces, they weren't. They reflected the work and thinking of a kinetic man, one who launched a historically important institution in the field of testing.

There were times when Jane, frustrated at not being able to find the right words or thoughts, would sit weeping at her typewriter. All I could do at those times would be to kiss her, hug her, and assure her to hang in there . . . she'd get it soon. She always did.

Henry Chauncey wanted Jane on the staff. When she agreed to his proposal, he assigned her the job of organizing a new publications division—and appointed her director. As usual, she did an excellent job, hiring a staff of capable people who systematically began the work of bringing order, planning, and quality to ETS publications.

This was perhaps her happiest time at ETS—in a job she could control and encompass in every way, while letting her talents for being wife, mother, and professional worker flourish. A local Princeton newspaper, the *Packet*, interviewed Jane in 1962. In that interview, Jane expressed how she was feeling about her life.

"I don't think I'm at all unusual," she said. "I know lots of Princeton women who combine three careers, happily busy at homemaking, child rearing and who also hold jobs they love. I guess we're living proof of the nationwide statistical fact that women, in steadily growing numbers, are working at all kinds of jobs."

The reporter described Jane's work attitude as "calm efficiency, a friendly smile, plenty of time for the needs of the moment coupled with a businesslike attitude of time is money—and a mind that considers problems and concepts with sensitivity and logical insight."

Jane told the reporter of son Guy's remark when he learned that the mother of one of his friends also worked at ETS. "It seems to me," he said, "that everybody's mother works at ETS."

"If I don't get my newspaper reading done in the evening, I feel abused," said Jane.

"So what do you do with your spare time?" the reporter asked.

"Oh, the marketing, cooking, errands to the cleaners, garage, and so forth. And all of us enjoy playing golf."

About ETS, Jane said in that interview, "This is a tremendously interesting and complex organization to work in. In one way or another, all of ETS's activities relate to most of the new trends in education, new curriculum developments, new efforts to solve old educational problems. It's the kind of place where you find each day, and each new project, more interesting and challenging than the one before."

Throughout our lives together, I'd helped Jane around the house and with the chores. When our sons were babies, I did the washing, which included hundreds of dirty diapers. But in retrospect, I could have done so much more, to have given her more precious time for herself. She never complained and always seemed happy. I, of course, was always immersed in my job. On weekends, as the boys were growing up, I taught them baseball, football, tennis, swimming, and later, golf. When they took care of their own games, I began to play golf with a foursome weekend mornings—and played another round with Jane Saturday and Sunday afternoons.

Still, in the later years, I never helped Jane enough. And I will always regret it.

6

The Mystery of Naloxone

Once again my hopes were raised at reading an article in a medical journal by Dr. Barry Riesberg, a neurologist at the New York University Medical Center. This was a few months after our year-long experiment with Praxilene at Albert Einstein College of Medicine. I was still looking for help for Jane.

I'd heard him speak at the monthly Alzheimer's disease meetings held at the Gracie Square Hospital on the Upper East Side. He was young, appeared to know a great deal about Alzheimer's, and seemed confident about himself and what he knew.

Dr. Riesberg's article seemed to promise an answer. In it, he told of success in treating seven Alzheimer's patients with a drug called Naloxone. This drug had been accepted by the Food and Drug Administration as a treatment for drug addicts. It was not approved for any other medical problem, although experimental programs like Dr. Riesberg's were routinely approved by the FDA.

I immediately sat down at the typewriter and wrote Dr.

Riesberg, asking to have Jane treated with Naloxone. I received a telephone response from a woman whose name I can't remember.

"Dr. Riesberg," she said, "is not administering the drug to anyone other than the patients in his program."

Again disappointment hit me, hard. I thought I was inured to such setbacks. But I realized it still hurt.

"But—if you're interested in having Mrs. Wirsig take this drug," she went on, "there is another way it can be done."

"Yes," I said, my hopes already rising. "I'd like to know."

"There is an Institute for the Aging," she said, giving me the address on the Upper East Side. "You can make an appointment to meet with a doctor and staff at the Institute to see if Mrs. Wirsig is acceptable for such a program."

I found the Institute in one of those apartment houses that have professional offices on the ground floor and residential apartments above.

Something about the setting made me uneasy. In a small, sparsely furnished outer office, a cheap sign reading INSTITUTE FOR THE AGING hung askew above the door. I didn't know whether we should knock first or just enter. I finally pushed the door open and saw a small anteroom with four chairs lined against the wall. A table was pushed against the other wall, near another door. On this table, with several lights blinking at once, was a professional telephone.

Nobody seemed to be there. I decided that Jane and I should sit down and wait, anyway. We sat. Some ten minutes later, the door opened and a woman came out of the inner office.

"Mr. and Mrs. Wirsig?" she asked.

"Yes," I said. "I don't know if this is the place we should be. . . ."

She did not smile or change expression. "You are here for the Naloxone?"

"We're here to explore the matter," I said, again feeling wary.

"The doctor will want to talk to you first," she said, as if she hadn't heard me. "He'll be free in a few minutes." She disappeared behind the door.

We waited another fifteen minutes. Just as we were about to get up and leave, the door opened again.

"The doctor can see you now. Won't you come in?"

We entered another small office, bare of anything except a desk and three chairs. Behind the desk sat a youthful man with tousled hair and a sad expression.

"You're here about Naloxone!" he said. It was not a question.

"Yes," I said. "That is, I want to explore it on behalf of Jane, my wife."

We talked for about fifteen minutes. The young man was a doctor, he said. And the woman was his assistant. Both were associated with Dr. Riesberg at the New York University Medical Center. But—and the "but" was unmistakable—the Institute for the Aging had no connection with either Dr. Riesberg or the New York University Medical Center. The Institute was a private organization set up to administer Naloxone to some patients who might benefit from it.

"Naloxone is a drug accepted by the Food and Drug Administration for treatment of drug addicts under certain circumstances," the young doctor explained. "When administered carefully, by someone who understands it, it is a safe drug. There has been some success with it in treating some patients with Alzheimer's disease. . . ."

"Yes," I said. "That's why we're here"

I gave him Jane's history while he took notes. Then he said they would accept Jane on an experimental basis.

By this time I was heartsick and ready to flee. What had I gotten us into? I hadn't talked this over with either Dr. Stone or Dr. Fulmer. Surely they would look suspiciously at the whole matter, especially the rather mysterious and—what seemed to me, anyway— unorthodox manner in which the drug was to be administered.

Still, we were there. And I was stubborn. A stream of pros and cons swept through my mind. I finally decided we'd go through with it. The doctor listened to Jane's heart. He took her blood pressure. Then he led us into another little room that contained an examining table. He asked Jane to lie down on the table. Then he inject her with a hypodermic needle just above the elbow. The injection must not have hurt, for Jane didn't wince. She took it serenely, as if it were just another one of those crazy things that people were doing to her these days.

"We'll see how she tolerates the injection," the doctor said, holding a wrist while listening to her pulse. Then he listened to her heart again. A few minutes later he said we could leave.

The woman assistant reappeared in the doorway. "That will be a hundred dollars," she said. "We would like you to pay it now, please."

I wrote out a check, surprised—and yet not very surprised—that they would not send us a bill, as would most medical offices.

"You have a receipt for me?" I asked. "Surely, this is reimbursible by Medicare and Mrs. Wirsig's insurance company?"

The woman hesitated, as if thinking over what she would say in reply. "Yes—yes," she said, finally. "It is completely reimbursible, as any treatment would be."

A few minutes later I had to remind her again for a receipt. "Yes. Yes," she said, flustered now. "We are just new and haven't such things printed yet. But I'll write out a receipt this way."

On a plain sheet of paper she wrote, "Received of Mrs. Wirsig $100," and signed her name.

"But this has no letterhead," I said. "And it doesn't say what it's all about. This will not be good enough for us."

"Um," she murmured. Then she wrote out another

receipt: "Received $100 for treatment by Naloxone," and signed the doctor's name as well as her own.

Reluctantly I accepted it, thinking it probably wouldn't be good enough for Medicare and the ETS health plan.

Then we made an appointment for the following month.

In my own mind I decided that this probably was a way for Dr. Riesberg and his associates at New York University Medical Center to profit privately from Naloxone—if it worked—without either sharing with too many others or experiencing too much liability. I don't know this for a fact; it's just speculation, but it seemed to be the only logical explanation for the cheap offices and the mysterious way they handled us.

At the next appointment, the doctor and his assistant asked Jane to take a test. "An oral test," they explained. "To see if there's any change."

A young man with glasses and a superior air explained that he was a psychologist and would administer a battery of tests to check on Jane's memory. I watched as he spread pictures and charts out in front of Jane and began asking her questions. I didn't pay much attention to what he was doing, for I wanted to watch Jane react. This was still relatively early in her illness, perhaps a year and a half or two after her diagnosis, although in retrospect I'm sure she had been becoming ill a number of years earlier. Jane was able to hear the young man's questions—and respond.

At each answer, the young man busily jotted down a symbol in a chart.

Again, as she had with several of the neurologists who had examined her, Jane grew exasperated with herself in trying to answer some of the questions. She knew she knew—or should know—the answers.

"Next time," the young man said, smiling, "we'll go over this same test to see if she will do better."

Next time, there was either no change in her responses—or she was even more confused.

I was disappointed and had to fight discouragement.

Jane had had six injections. I'd watched her carefully and could not detect any change—improvement or decline—in the way she talked or moved. After several more visits, I decided to quit this Naloxone program.

"Mr. Wirsig, we haven't seen Mrs. Wirsig in some time," the doctor's assistant said, calling me on the phone one day. "Do you wish to continue?"

"She doesn't seem to respond to the Naloxone," I said. "It just doesn't have any effect."

"It's still early, of course," she replied. There was a tentative note in her voice.

"Well, I may be making a mistake. A big mistake," I said. "But I think we won't have any more injections."

"I'm sorry," she said.

"I'm sorry, too," I said.

After the fact, I asked Dr. Leonard Stone about Naloxone. He questioned me closely about every detail.

Then he nodded. "Well, I guess it hasn't hurt Jane," he said. "I'm familiar with Naloxone. I don't see how it could have helped."

My own feelings were relief, coupled with resigned disappointment again. At least we didn't hurt Jane. Be thankful for that, I thought. Still, nothing so far seemed to work in the way I hoped.

Because the doctor's assistant's receipts were so confused, and confusing to me, I tried to reach her by phone and letter to get them straightened out. I suspect the Institute for the Aging didn't last very long. The phone never answers. And my letters to her were returned, addressee no longer at the address.

I never heard of the Institute for the Aging again.

As I think back, the period beginning at Henry Chauncey's retirement in 1970 was both the height of Jane's professional career—and the beginning of her difficulties.

Because of her excellent record as director of publications, Jane was promoted by the new ETS president, William Turnbull, to executive director of information services. Jane was pleased because it meant another step upward. Now publications as well as public relations and all information services were under her direction.

Jane was a good, thoughtful administrator. People enjoyed working for her because she was fair, forthright, and understanding. But now, in retrospect, I think Jane was beginning to suffer the earliest inroad of Alzheimer's disease.

There were times, in her work, when she needed to make forceful decisions. Reluctantly, she would make them, often after talking them over with me. But I had the feeling that she was needlessly and unusually soft in her approach to some executive situations. Not that she was soft in her thinking; as always, Jane's mind was sharp and to the point. But sometimes I felt she was explaining her thoughts and positions in terms too soft and passive to inspire the kind of alert, assertive action she needed.

Several of her staff, I felt, particularly in public relations and special writing, tended to bully her. This, of course, infuriated me. Such bullying should never have been tolerated.

Jane, however, seemed to make do. The work got done. I can remember times, however, when she would almost weep at her frustrations over some staff member's reluctance to do the work.

A former associate of Jane's had this to say about her abilities:

"Jane was certainly among the brightest and ablest people I've ever known. I still remember those days in 1960 when she fought off those political attacks from people at ETS who opposed the formation of the publications division. Building a publishing arm and then a public relations division in the span of—what was it, fifteen years?—is extraordinary by any standards. ETS should be very grateful to her."

Not long after Bill Turnbull became ETS president, the position of corporate secretary opened up. Jane was appointed to the position, a move that pleased everyone who knew her and pleased Jane herself.

During her first few years as corporate secretary, Jane did her usual excellent job. She was admired and beloved by the members of the Board of Trustees. Jane's quiet sense of humor, her perceptive handling of their views as expressed in letters, memoranda, and on the telephone, and her accurate and literate minutes of the Board meetings always brought words of praise from ETS executives and Board members themselves.

Jane enjoyed being a member of a team, whether as one of the troops or as a captain. When she was particularly proud of what her staff accomplished, she would tell them—often conveying her deep thoughts in a light vein.

After her staff completed a particularly difficult task one time, Jane addressed this memo to the staff members:

To: Bobbi   Loretta
      Elise   Marguerite
      Jane   Vi
      Joan   Vivian

How can I thank you for all that you've done,
For that one hectic week when you were all on the run?
You checked and retyped and handled the phone,
There was hardly a moment you could grasp as your own.

The phones, how they rang; and the forms, how they grew.
There was no escaping, there was so much to do.
The inquiries, the buses, the myriad details,
You fielded them all and still came the mails.

The IC was bigger than ever 'twas dreamed.
There were 600 plus, though thousands it seemed.

Pre-registered ones had their tag and lunch ticket,
Though hectic it was, you really stuck with it.

Vivian, Jane, Vi, Marguerite, and Joan
Worked feet and fingers right to the bone.
Elise, Loretta, and Bobbi were beckoned
And worked harder and longer than anyone reckoned.

You all were so busy and each lent a hand.
You were pushed to the limit and were, in a word, grand.
And you smiled and you worked too hard to believe
That you could work harder still when you did so indeed.

You really deserve all the praise I can heap,
But I fear virtue is the only reward you will reap.
You've done yeoman's service with aplomb and with class,
So pretend this toasting is with champagne and stemmed glass.

With gratitude and poetic license
JW

Another time, when Jane was moving upstairs at Conant Hall, the ETS administration building, to be among the other executives, her staff threw a little party. Jane penned this to them:

AN ODE (sort of) to
Amy/Ann/Betsy/Fran/Gloria/Peter/Rita/Vivian

'Though I can't be a poet,
Pen a rhyme or a sonnet,
I'm taking the time
To say you're all just fine.

What a group we had at the Smith Eatery

On July 1 this year—good friends past and present,
Friendly, able folk surrounded by Smith greenery—
A milestone to be remembered long past the moment!

Super is the word for each and every one.
It fits all of you to a "T," and then some.
How could I be lucky enough to choose
Those who toasted me in Cold Duck booze?

Upstairs or down, this boss knows
That she's got the best staff in town.
Together, we can put on real good shows
And perhaps be dubbed as a group of renown!

> (composed, typed, and proofed
> by some obscure amateur who
> was moved to try her hand at
> verse instead of sticking to her
> own trade)

> P.S.   No corporate seal required
> on this document. Date:
> July 1, 1974.

> JW

This time, her staff answered in kind on a "Quickie-Note," an interoffice memorandum form:
DATE: July 1, 1974
TO: JW
SUBJECT: On Moving Upstairs
Oh, JW, JW.
We're sorry to trouble you.
But please take the time
(in spite of our rhyme)
To hear this awful Quicki-Note
That, for all of us, I quickly wrote.
We just want you to know
Wherever you go
That whether you're upstairs

Or possibly down
We think that your bosshood's
the best in this town.
                    Most sincerely (although with a laugh)
                    FROM: Your double-decker Conant Hall staff

But the work became more demanding as the ETS law-
yers insisted that minutes not be recorded and edited.
Rather, the minutes should be taken down in longhand
notes—to reflect general attitudes rather than specific
comments. The reason: to protect the trustees against nuisance suits, investigations, and controversy.

Jane, who had always been able to take excellent notes,
handled the challenge well—until her illness began to
overtake her.

This was a period I wish I could live over. I was wrapped
up in my new customer services/consumer affairs audit
business—a procedure I'd developed at the Better Business Bureau. My associates and I would examine a company's customer services and consumer affairs activities from
the chairman down to the bottom of the hierarchy, mea-
suring each aspect against objective criteria. We were
auditing major corporations, taking us to Southern California, Arizona, and other states, sometimes for three or four
weeks at a time.

To be sure, I'd talk to Jane each evening on the phone.
Her voice would be strong and buoyant. We would tell
each other how much we loved each other. But I don't
know how well she was eating, what confusing thoughts
may have begun to trouble her, how discouraged she may
have been.

How I wish, now, that I had not been away from home
at all.

As I think back, there were a number of signs that Jane
was not herself. All through our lives together, up to then,
Jane almost never complained about anything. Whenever
she had strong feelings about something, she made her

point positively. But then she began to complain about matters that never would have bothered her before. She began to criticize her family for small errors. One early evening, for example, Jane's sister Nancy was late for a six o'clock dinner that Jane had prepared. Before, Jane would simply have kept the meal warm in the oven. This time, she chewed Nancy out for her thoughtlessness for being late. At the time, Nancy thought it strange—but said nothing.

In our conversations, Jane began to ask me questions that made we wonder. That is, her questions were increasingly on tangents off our main subject. Sometimes I realized that her questions were slightly skewed. I dismissed it as another part of her increasingly critical attitude. I should add that what I describe as Jane's critical attitude would, in others, be regarded as normal. She was nowhere near the cantankerous state that many, if not most, Alzheimer's victims reach.

My son, Guy, brought me up agonizingly short one day during a visit from his home in California.

"Dad," he said, "it seems that you're in a perpetual state of anger toward Mom."

That was a shock to me. I never felt such anger. At first I couldn't believe he was right. But I soon realized that my responses to Jane's changing nature must have made it seem that I was angry at her all the time. How terrible! How really terrible! I never, absolutely never, had reason to be angry at Jane. The remorse is still with me—and always will be.

"I wish," Jane said to me one day, "I could pick out my clothes the night before. The way you do. In the morning, when I'm hurrying to get to work, I just thrash around trying to decide what to wear."

Jane continued to do our accounts during this period. I noticed that she always needed her calculator, however. Whenever it was on the blink she postponed her accounts until it was fixed.

It seemed strange to me, although I dismissed it from my mind almost at once, that Jane kept buying new bottles of Oil of Olay until she had perhaps eight or ten full bottles in her medicine cabinet. True, the marketing appeal of Oil of Olay must have been compelling to women. But as I thought about it later, it seemed unutterably sad that Jane sought some elusive beauty through a bottle of something she could buy—and again, I realized that I should have, could have, really wanted to, tell her more often how truly beautiful she was to me.

A change in Jane's pattern of entertaining was one indication that something was happening to her, although I was not aware of it then. I tend to emphasize Jane's professional accomplishments because I'm so proud of her abilities and what she has done. At the same time, I've always been conscious of how superb a homemaker she always was, a warm and loving wife to me and mother to our three sons.

We enjoyed our friends and going out on social occasions. And Jane liked to cook for our dinner parties. We weren't "social," in the sense that we simply had to have engagements for every weekend. It seemed to me that we were contented and serene in our pattern of living.

We would have friends in for dinner and an evening rather frequently, even though Jane never thought of herself as a particularly good cook. Friends did say, however, that her roast turkeys at Thanksgiving and Christmas, and her scalloped potatoes, for example, were the best they'd ever tasted. She could produce a dinner for eight or sixteen without trauma, get the boys fed and ready for bed, and still be able to sit down for a pre-dinner cocktail.

Then it began to change. And the change was so subtle that it went on, and increased, for perhaps several years before I realized there was a change. Jane's entertaining became less and less frequent. Then she stopped having dinner parties altogether.

At first, when I thought about it, I felt perhaps she was

tired. Since I enjoy evenings at home with her, burying myself in the newspapers and in books, I didn't care and rarely thought about it. Once in a while I'd realize that our lovely linens, our simple silverware, and the beautiful Loewy-designed china remained stored away in cabinets. But I didn't care.

Suddenly, during this period, Jane decided to have a small dinner party. Even though her corporate secretary work was complex, and increasingly difficult, Jane planned the dinner and carried it out.

She knew it was something special for me—and, as usual, wanted to do it for me. The director of my Occidental College Men's Glee Club, Howard Swan, and his wife were in Princeton that summer for concerts with the Williamson Choir College. Swan, retired from Occidental, was highly regarded throughout the nation—indeed, the world—as a choir and glee club conductor. And the Williamson Choir College had him back as often as possible.

Swan had been particularly good to me when I transferred from UCLA to Occidental and needed work to pay my tuition. Swan put me to work in the college news bureau. As a student, I was encouraged to try out for the Men's Glee Club. I'd sung second tenor in high school and several church choirs. But I wasn't at all sure I could cut it with the famous Oxy Men's Glee Club.

The day I tried out, Swan knew I was nervous and tense. So at one point he told me to hold two chairs out at arms' length from my body—and then sing the scales. He must have seen, or heard, something there—for he entered me into the Men's Glee Club as a first tenor, no less, and I sang for him for two years.

Jane knew it would please me to have them over for dinner. She prepared a delicious meal. She set the table with her pale green tablecloth, napkins to match, candles to be lighted as we sat down, and then she began serving.

She served vichyssoise, a delicious veal dish with carrots, peas, and broccoli. Her salad consisted of endive, lettuce, tomatoes, peppers, celery, and cucumber. Then there was vanilla ice cream, with a topping of crème de menthe or crème d' cacao. And coffee. It was as perfect as one could get, in my opinion. We talked into the night.

From beginning to end, it was a superb dinner party—and Jane did it at a time when surely the Alzheimer's illness was taking hold and marring her self-confidence.

Despite such successes, one experience at least should have shown me that something serious was wrong. I wanted to teach Jane how to drive my new little station car, a stick-shift Chevette. As a girl, Jane had learned how to drive a stick-shift auto and it held no mysteries for her. During the previous eight years or so, she drove my stick-shift Kharman Ghia. But the Chevette was slightly different—requiring the clutch to be depressed to start the car. And its gear-shift was different from the Ghia.

To teach her, we would go again and again to the nearby shopping center, where spacious parking areas, left empty on Sundays, provided space for practice driving. It was there I had taught our three sons to drive.

I would take Jane through the motions, then turn the car over to her. Each time she would forget to do something in the sequence. Either she forgot to depress the clutch while starting the car, or she couldn't remember the shifting sequence, she would forget to depress the clutch while shifting. Something went wrong each time.

Jane could see how she was disappointing me. And that upset her. True, whenever I cannot see some reasonable explanation for a problem I tend to get impatient. I'm sure there were times when I was exasperated, for it was important in the way we ran our household for Jane to be able to drive both of our cars. It never occurred to me, of course, to get another automatic transmission for her sake.

I finally gave up trying to teach her. Jane never did learn to drive the Chevette. This should have been another warning.

She began to look tired. Had I had my wits about me I'd have noticed other problem indications. One evening, she came home shaken and upset, her face ashen. She had been weeping, I could tell. I'd never seen Jane so disturbed.

"It was awful," she said, clinging to me as I took her in my arms to hold her. "Just awful."

"Tell me, darling," I said. "What was awful?"

"Bob Solomon," she started to say. "He—he talked terribly to me today. It was awful."

I kissed and hugged her, murmuring that I loved her. And to try to tell me what happened.

"He called me into his office to talk about the Board's minutes," she said. "He said they were incomplete. So many mistakes were made. They would have to be done over, he said. And he was so—so brutal about it."

"The sonofabitch," I muttered. He was the ETS executive vice president to whom Jane reported, now that Turnbull was president.

"I went in to see Bill Turnbull," she went on, drying her eyes, some spunk coming back into her voice. "He told me not to worry, that Bob Solomon was just on edge about something else these days. That made me feel a little better."

I heard the end of that particular story years later, long after Jane's illness was known to everybody. The senior vice president Scarvia Anderson, a good friend of Jane's, told me of her conversation with Bob Solomon.

"Solomon was telling me, 'Jane must be stupid, or ignorant, or something.' And I told him, 'Jane is not stupid. She's not ignorant. She's a brilliant person. She must be ill or something.'"

It's just as well that I didn't hear Solomon's comment to Scarvia Anderson at the time or I'd have done something to him, something drastic. . . .

That winter of 1980 was dark and cold. Days were long and dreary. I felt that it might be a good idea for Jane and me to take a winter trip to Hawaii. We hadn't done that sort of thing much.

Jane calmly went along with me in deciding to go. I asked her, several times, whether she could leave her work. It would be between Board meetings and all her correspondence should be caught up. Surely, I thought, she should be able to go, having always given more than was ever called for in anything she undertook. At the time, I didn't notice that she didn't seem to express much enthusiasm for the trip. There was none of the excitement or anticipation that she usually showed when we planned a trip.

We flew off to Hawaii on a rather luxurious tour of the islands, staying in the most expensive hotels, eating expensive meals, being transported in limousines.

Jane and I were together. Slowly, she began to love the trip. She was curious about everything and seemed to enjoy every aspect of the tour.

She marveled at the greenness of the mountains, at the beauty and luxuriant qualities of the flowers. We did all the touristy things. We visited Pearl Harbor and other sights on Oahu, then flew to Kauai. There we took a helicopter ride over the island, dropping down on the beach at the northwestern end. There, at the bottom of steep cliffs, the surf was pounding and lifting higher than a house, thundering against the rocks and sand with a noise that made Jane uneasy.

The tour included drives about the island, river trips, and rides up to the tops of volcanos, passing from tropical heat to freezing temperatures. Jane trudged along with me, plucky in every aspect, with never a word of complaint or fatigue.

On the big island of Hawaii, we drove out to the large active volcano, then drove down into and across it. The steam frightened Jane, but she stuck with me to marvel at how large the crater was. Since then, of course, the volcano has erupted a number of times, spewing molten lava down the sides of the mountain and wreaking destruction.

I did notice that she seemed somewhat more quiet and reflective than usual, although being quiet and reflective is her general nature. She ate well, although slowly, as usual. Still, I thought she was enjoying the trip and would go back to ETS with some renewed enthusiasm. We danced, and played golf, and thoroughly enjoyed ourselves.

During our return, we stopped in Denver to have a between-the-planes dinner with my brother Alan and his wife. Later, Alan told me, "Jane just looks awful. Is she sick?"

Only a few months later came one of the most poignant moments Jane and I ever experienced together. It was time for the June Board of Trustees dinner meeting, prior to its regular meeting. These dinners, held in the Henry Chauncey Conference Center's luxurious dining rooms, were always enjoyable for both of us. I particularly enjoyed watching Jane's organizational handiwork—and seeing how highly the Board members regarded her.

But suddenly, as I was about to get ready to go with her, as usual, she turned to me with a strange look on her face. Her manner was unusually awkward. She was obviously embarrassed and was trying to shrug it off with nonchalance.

"Darling," she said, hesitantly, "I'd rather—you—you didn't come with me tonight."

True, I was shocked—but the shock was immediately mixed with deep concern about what was behind her unusual request.

"Sure—sure, sweetheart," I said quickly. Then I took her in my arms and kissed her. "Is something wrong?"

She was limp, unresponsive, and seemed about to weep —but she managed a small smile. "No, nothing's wrong especially. It just won't be very interesting, that's all."

I let it go. Something was really the matter, but she obviously didn't want to tell me—at least not then. So off she went to the dinner. And I buried myself in the newspapers and TV, waiting for her to come home.

How I wish I could have sensed, then, the agony that must have been going on inside her. She must have known this would be her last meeting . . . and that perhaps something would happen that would embarrass me, or somehow demean her in my estimation.

When Jane returned home after the Board dinner, she showed me a letter composed by Turnbull and signed by all the members of the Board. I read it with some surprise, and rising anger—yet, somehow, deep down, I wasn't surprised. I had felt that something like this was coming. I noticed, considering the truly distinguished work Jane had accomplished through the years, that the letter conveyed "routine" thanks and appreciation after a resignation. Perhaps I'm especially sensitive to anything that anyone might do to hurt Jane, but it seemed to me to be the kind of retiring boilerplate that could have applied to most anyone who had not run off with the company's payroll. That, I quickly realized, was an uncharitable thought—for Bill Turnbull was genuinely brilliant and from beginning to end was a loyal champion of Jane and her abilities as well as a loyal friend. He would have done his best in such a letter.

Jane's voice held a sense of relief, as if a weight had been lifted from her back. "I'll keep my office," she said, "and from now on I report to Scarvia." That, at least, was gratifying to me. In other words, Jane was not fired. That would have been devastating to her, as it is to most. Instead, she would be an executive-at-large with unspecified duties.

I feel the agony even now. Those months, possibly even years, of silent stress and mental turmoil, wondering about herself, knowing something must be wrong, but what? Not knowing what it was or what to do . . . causing, finally, an ulcer, a response to her stress.

Almost without realizing what she was doing, Jane cut

down her time at the office. Without anything specific to do, without responsibility—without, in fact, being able to do anything—she would go in late, about 10 A.M., and come home in the early afternoon.

I reported the results of her neurological tests to Bill Turnbull. What could we do, I asked, to determine that Jane was totally disabled? I knew there would be some kind of disability benefits through ETS's health coverage plan and its retirement program.

Then I began the paperwork to establish that Jane was totally disabled for Social Security. I had feared this process, having little regard for any bureaucracy. But I must admit that in this case at least I was wrong. The papers, while long and asking a great number of questions, and requiring signatures of her various physicians, were appropriate for establishing her disability.

It was a major step—taking Jane from a healthy, productive worker to the status of a totally disabled person, unable to work or take care of herself . . . a designation to last forever.

Finally, we were required to have Jane examined by a neurologist designated by the Social Security system. I will always remember that experience.

The neurologist was busy and brusque. Jane undressed, donned an examining smock, and sat waiting. She was patient. At last the neurologist called her in. I asked if I could be with her.

"I'd appreciate being able to sit in," I said to him. "She may need me to help her."

"Sure, sure," he said. "Doesn't matter."

He gave Jane a brief physical, to see that she was not disabled in any physical way.

Then he began the questions.

"Count backward for me, starting with 97," he said.

Jane replied, "My name is Jane. I live in Princeton. . . ."

Startled, the neurologist repeated his question. "Count backward, Mrs. Wirsig," he said.

Jane repeated, "My name is Jane. I live in Princeton. . . ." Her voice was calm, even placid. She felt she was responding to his questions.

Flustered, he took another tack. "Tell me your last name?"

"My name is Jane," she replied. "I live in Princeton."

I could see how frustrated the neurologist was. However, he was busy. He came to his conclusion swiftly. He stopped the examination and, brusquely, told Jane to get dressed.

To me, he said with a short wave of his hand, "I'm sorry. She has Alzheimer's. I'm sure she cannot work or take care of herself. She will be designated as totally disabled.

Again, my emotions were mixed, sadness tempered with relief that Jane would receive total disability benefits from Social Security—how much I didn't know. With disability benefits from ETS and from Social Security, and my own pensions and deferred salary, we would have enough to continue living in our Princeton townhouse—and I could take care of her.

Then I became even busier.

Jane was beginning to show another of the Alzheimer's physical symptoms: incontinence. To cope, I studied the different incontinent garments. I finally settled on Procter & Gamble's Attends.

I decided not to waken her in the middle of the night to take her to the toilet. Instead, I would diaper her well—and let her sleep. Then I would be sure to bathe her each morning before dressing for the day. At night, I covered her hips and thighs with baby oil to protect against her urine. This way, I thought, she could sleep through the night and still not harm her skin.

And so I, too, could sleep through the night.

I kept reading everything I could get about Alzheimer's. The more I read, the more depressed I got. But I went on. I had to know what was ahead of us.

I also began attending a series of weekly lectures at the

Gracie Square Hospital. The speakers spoke on topics across the range of Alzheimer's problems. Some talks focused on the caregiver, which with some surprise I realized included me.

I learned, for example, that I should obtain a power of attorney as soon as possible, and that I should switch as much of our property into my name as possible—as soon as possible.

Above all, I learned, I should persuade Jane to stop driving her car. She could hurt herself terribly in an accident—and possibly hurt others. And the practical logic was inescapable. If Jane should have an accident, and kill or injure someone, the damages could wipe us out. Although we have good liability insurance, I knew there would be a coverage problem if Jane were driving while disabled.

An incident dramatized how urgent it was to stop her driving. One day, as she was driving alone, she backed slowly out of a parking lot. Confused, she tried to tell me later what happened. From what I pieced together, she slightly bumped a car behind her. It was barely a touch. Always a good driver, Jane was upset. I could visualize the scene: The male driver of the car was undoubtedly angry. He probably demanded Jane's insurance slip. She probably tried to respond but was unable to understand . . . or get out her insurance form. The damage to the other car, however, was so slight—and the insurance company was so willing to pay the damages—that there was no problem. That time.

But I knew there must not be a next time.

Naturally, I worried about taking her car away from her. A car, and being able to drive it anywhere, anytime, meant independence. But I needn't have been concerned. Persuading Jane to stop driving was easy. It just happened naturally, somehow. She simply ceased to want to drive. Willingly, she let me drive her everywhere.

I turned in her driver's license.

Jane's Social Security benefit checks began coming. At

the same time, TIAA/CREF, the pension system for ETS employees, began sending disability benefits—while continuing her monthly payments into the pension system. Technically, she remained an ETS employee. Even though Jane was designated as totally disabled, she remained as an active employee for five years. During that time she received disability benefits and payments into her pension, until her formal retirement in March 1986.

Our lives fell into a simple routine. Some time ago I'd taken over the job of handling our accounts. At the time, I feared the incessant details. But I rather quickly figured out my own routine—and it works.

I cook breakfast, prepare lunch, cook dinner. I began to prepare simple meals, mostly free of fat and salt and cholesterol, yet with good nutrition. Our big oven baffled me. So I got a microwave oven, which served my purposes in excellent fashion.

For breakfast, I'd fix Jane two soft-boiled eggs, a dish of whole-grain cereal, and one slice of whole-grain bread toast with her favorite, orange marmalade, on it. Milk, a banana, and three prunes finished the meal.

For lunch I'd fix her a peanut butter sandwich on whole-grain bread. Then, a glass of milk and some fruit.

For dinner, we'd have a meat that she liked, usually chicken, ham, or ground beef. Once in a while, I'd fix one of the good frozen dinners. All my vegetables were frozen, but I figured these were nutritious enough for both of us. I'd bake potatoes, usually choose two vegetables from among broccoli, cauliflower, carrots, peas, beans, corn—and fix a salad.

Try as I would, I could never make a small salad. Cutting up lettuce, celery, tomatoes, peppers, apples, sometimes tofu, sometimes endive, always seemed to produce six times as much salad as we could consume at one sitting. When I began to fix her meals, I didn't know whether the salad could be saved for another day. But I began to experiment. If I didn't put salad dressing on it, I could save it for the next day. Through such experimenting, I began to learn how to save and use leftovers.

I disliked cooking. I did not under any circumstances want to spend the time to become a good cook. All I wanted to do was serve Jane something that would keep her healthy—as healthy as possible—and that she would like.

Perhaps I pushed too much food at Jane, still fearing that she wouldn't eat enough on her own to maintain her weight. It wasn't long before Jane got up to 144 pounds.

"Well," said Dr. Thal, "that's about it. I wouldn't let her get any heavier. Again, though, this is not bad at all. And remember—the time will come, sad to say, when we'll wish she would be able to gain weight."

I began to fear trouble with Jane's eating behavior. She was forgetting to use her fork or spoon. She would take a bite of food, put down her fork—and seem to forget to eat any more. I began to put the fork in her hand. At times, I would lift a spoonful to her mouth. Soon, I thought to myself, I will have to begin feeding her.

Most of the time I dressed Jane in slacks, a blouse, walking shoes, and socks. These were the easiest for me to wash and keep looking decent. Her blouses and slacks were wash-and-wear. They dried well without ironing. As a kid, in high school, I used to press my trousers—but in all the years I've been taking care of Jane I have yet to pick up an iron.

To this day I take Jane every week to have her hair done by Anthony—who has cared for her hair each week for the last twenty-five years. Every two months or so he colors her hair and gives her a permanent. I can never remember which comes first. I guess he does the permanent first, otherwise the permanent would affect the color. Still, in my mind, is the fear that somehow the chemicals from coloring her hair through the years may have caused her Alzheimer's. Dr. Pfeiffer thinks that hair coloring can cause Alzheimer's, especially if there is aluminum in it. But

Anthony refers to hundreds, even thousands, of other women who use the same chemicals and have healthy brains.

Not long after her diagnosis, Jane began to get up from her dryer at the beauty parlor and wander around before her hair was dry. This worried Anthony, more because he was concerned about Jane than because it upset his routine. He was pleased, though, when I said I'd stay with her while her hair was being done so that she'd be no problem. I would sit in a dryer chair beside Jane, holding her hand, while we waited for her hair to dry. She rarely tried to talk. When she did, her words tumbled out incoherently.

Jane knows when her hair looks good and when it doesn't. I often think that getting a shampoo and set is better therapy than anything else she does. Often, during the day, her hands will go up to her hair to pat and straighten it. In these movements, then and for many years afterward, the hands that touched her hair were as sure and graceful as they had been when she was well.

From time to time I'd write letters to Alan, Guy, and Paul, sending copies of the same letter to each. Sometimes I'd copy my mother, sometimes our longtime friend Harold Baron, of whom Jane was so fond. I sent this letter in 1983:

Dear Alan, Guy, Paul, and Mom:

I like the idea of sitting down and writing all of you at once. I often wish it could be a conversation. But since that's not in the cards, this is the better alternative. I want to find the time to do it more often.

Mainly I'm going to talk about Jane. I haven't really decided how to do it so I'll just start. I think you ought to know what is happening, what the status is, what the prognosis is. I'll try to report factually, but you know all about how I feel behind the words I say.

First of all, Jane feels that she is very happy. Every evening, as we sit down before the television set to have a glass of wine and watch the early news, she reaches over and takes my hand, smiles that sweet, wonderful smile of hers, and tells me how much she loves me and how happy she is. Of course, from the moment she wakens in the morning until we say good night, she tells me that she loves me. I know that she knows precisely what she's saying and why, and she says it precisely. She means it, I know. But she also is seeking reassurance. And I give it to her, with kisses, every time.

Physically she seems to be healthier than I can ever remember. For about a year now her weight has been a steady 128—and her figure looks better and fuller than ever before. While I'm making sure she eats, and eats well, I think it's the vitamin regimen she's on that's doing it. Her complexion is clear, her skin looks good, she sleeps well, she has vigor and doesn't take naps in the afternoon. To be sure, she starts dozing about 8:30 in the evening, but she revives and enjoys watching Merv at 9 P.M. Then to bed.

Yesterday we had our every-three-months visit with the neurologist at Albert Einstein College of Medicine. He said it simply: Jane had deteriorated substantially since he last saw her three months ago. And at that time he said she had substantially deteriorated since the time previous. I may have told you that the last time we'd seen him three months ago he told me that within eighteen months she would lose all word facility—and probably begin having incontinence problems. Well, the word-facility loss is already here. I'll speak more about it later.

The neurologist, who is a young man, tells me that it is very important that I continue to have a very active life outside the home and apart from Jane. He says this with some personal insistence, based, I suspect, on the fact that his mother has had a chronic illness most of her life and his father reduced his life to her level—and, he says, it was bad. I tell you this simply because this is what he is insisting upon.

As I've said, I don't really mind closing down and around Jane. I've really had an exciting and wonderful professional life, filled with all the ego-fulfilling things I could ever ask for. And I'll probably do a lot of writing at home. So I don't really mind the idea of curtailing things more and more to take care of Jane. We'll see how it goes.

Now, however, to tell you how she is:

When she gets up in the morning, Jane dislikes taking a shower. I have to help her into the shower, put the soap on a wash-rag, soap her, rinse her, soap her feet. She does towel herself dry. But unless I lay out her clothes, she will keep on wearing the same old dirty clothes she wore the day before—and the day before that, if I don't lay out clean ones.

I meant to start this section with my belief that from the moment she wakens, her lifelong habits of doing the right things, doing good work, and doing things for others go into operation . . . only her poor brain fouls up everything. Nothing works right. She will put on two blouses. She will put on slacks while wearing a slip. She does not like to have me put her dirty clothes into a hamper to be ready for washing on the weekend, although her protest is not a resentment of me but my interrupting a pattern she has established for herself—not realizing that it's not what she thinks it is.

At breakfast she can no longer understand the words I speak when I suggest that she get out the coffee cups and spoon out the coffee. Instead, she will pick up the car keys or her glasses. In setting the breakfast table, she will take out ten spoons and no knives or forks. Or she will put down four napkins at each place. Trying so hard to do what's right. . . .

Whenever I fix her scrambled eggs, she tends to want to spoon the eggs onto her toast. I ask her not to do this because I know she wants to eat out with friends or in their homes. And she herself doesn't want to have bad habits. She tends to spoon orange marmalade out with a fork. There are times when her she has spooned some egg on her toast and I ask her not to, then she takes her fork in one hand and toast in the other—and you can see her brain trying to tell her what to do, which to put in her mouth first . . . all the time wanting so much to do the right thing, and to make me happy and pleased with her. I am gentle and quiet with her; I really am. If it takes ten or twenty times to ask her to use a spoon or a fork or a knife, I do it quietly and gently. And she doesn't seem to mind.

Taking her vitamins has become a terrible chore. It's hard for her to put a vitamin in her mouth then take a drink of milk or water to swallow it. And she has about twenty-five to take each morning and the same number at night, including her high blood pressure pill and Praxilene. Sometimes she weeps at the thought of taking them. Sometimes, not often, perhaps once every six weeks, she will heave up her breakfast and whatever vitamins she's taken. She's sorry about this because she feels she has failed me. I encourage her and hold her and kiss her and reassure her and it seems to calm her down.

She enjoys going to the hairdresser and to Brain Bio once a week. But her hairdresser was frantic until about two months ago, for Jane would get up from the dryer and start wandering around, looking for me. Finally I decided that I would simply wait for her while at the hairdresser. This quiets her and satisfies her. But it's wonderful to watch her at the hairdresser and Brain Bio. She loves people so much and feels so at ease and at home with them. She sparkles and says "Good morning," and "hello," or tries to—and enjoys their smiles. They *all* love her, take care of her carefully, as if she were some fragile piece of china. At Brain Bio, the girls in the lab who give her her B-12 shots come out, smile at her, and say "Jane, we're ready now." Jane goes up to them, smiling, confident, serene . . . they put an arm around her and lead her toward the room . . . and my heart just breaks.

Thus far, her lack of word facility doesn't hamper us much around the house. So much of her habits remain that when I start to do something, or demonstrate making the bed, or doing the washing, or taking out the trash, or whatever, she tries to help as much as she can. And she always wants to help and do what she can.

To help her feel useful and that she's helping me, I try to have some kind of envelope stuffing to do—either for ourselves, directly, or some survey for one of our clients. But it's getting to the point where even the simplest task is beyond her. The other day Bronwyn, the college girl I've hired to stay with Jane when I'm out of the house, and Jane were folding and inserting letters into envelopes while I was doing something else. I noticed something wrong with the way Jane was doing it. So I went over again . . . and again . . . and again to help her go through it. Finally, weeping quietly, she said, "I don't think I can do it." It's this kind of realization in her that just breaks my heart, more than anything else, because it has to do with pride, the fact that the college girl is there doing it easily, and the fact that she may be letting me down and not helping me as she wants to. I held her in my arms and reassured her again and again, then I sat down and stuffed the envelopes and gave them to her to put in a box. This she did—and felt better, as if she were helping me.

Having Bronwyn there has been very difficult. I can only suspect what the complex problems are. In the first place, Jane cannot imagine having her there to be with her. So she must be there to help me with the work, fixing up the files, etc., etc. So—if the girl is not down in the office working from the moment she arrives, Jane begins telling her to get to work. She resents it if Bronwyn comes upstairs to be with her. And those times when

Jane will put on her coat and start walking downtown and Bronwyn follows and catches up, Jane seems to resent it—not because she feels she's being spied upon, but because she thinks the girl is not doing her work for me.

Jane's behavior during the day is becoming more and more erratic. She will suddenly dart out of the house to look inside a car parked in front, or a neighbor's car, or to go hunting for me up the street. She is always looking for me.

She loves to go out to dinner. She loves to go out for breakfast at the Nassau Inn. She loves to go out with friends . . . although this is becoming a problem. Harold and Elizabeth seem to be the only ones who realize that it is important to include Jane in the conversation. And they do. And she loves being with them. With others, though, the tendency is to talk with me—about things Jane cannot comprehend or follow. And she feels left out. And, in feeling left out, she begins to get quite testy and wants to leave or go home. On the other hand, I've taken her to Westfield twice in the last few weeks to have an evening work meeting with my associates—and she sits at the table and listens, without interrupting once, for three hours—and says, on the way home, that she enjoyed it. And I know she did. So—she knows the difference between a meeting on things we're rassling with . . . and a friendly conversation that could include her. I think she even comprehends some of the things that go on in our meetings, although she couldn't even begin to repeat them. She can't even pronounce Bob's and Carolyn's and Gordon's names. However, she feels she's participating—is valued for herself. And this is important to her.

I think there's a good possibility of organizing a day-care center for Alzheimer's patients in Princeton. The reason I want one is so that Jane can be with other people who will chatter. I simply cannot chatter—and she cannot follow any kind of conversation unless it's my telling her I love her. Yet she tries to please me at all times.

Bronwyn is costing me about $210 a week. This on top of our cleaning lady begins to add up. I don't mind, really, because Jane likes our cleaning lady very much, and I think she's beginning to tolerate Bronwyn and may even begin to like her sometime soon.

The other afternoon, we went to see *The Verdict*, with Paul Newman. Jane sort of prattled through it, softly— but every once in a while I had to shush her. She didn't understand the story, of course, but she understood enough of the mood, the tension, the good people and the bad people, so that she was intensely moved— and afterward she said, "I thought it was wonderful. I liked it so much."

Several weeks ago, during the weekend of the big snow, we went to the Harlem Dance Theater with Harold, and Jane seemed to like that very much. She either understands it or enjoys the moods that are created.

It is always pleasant to drive with her somewhere, even though she tends to ask over and over and over again, incessantly, where we're going. But she enjoys beauty—and she is aware of things everywhere. An airplane going up at Newark Airport is something she enjoys and exclaims about. She always enjoys seeing the flight tower at Newark as a landmark she recognizes. She loves the beauty of the moon, whether it's an eyelash or full. She loves the beauty of a sunset. She loves to watch babies and little children. I often think that one of the things that would be good for her would be to go to a nursery and sit and watch the children.

We're getting ready to go to The Breakers next week. So, last night I did something that I've never done before—and I guess I wish I had done it more often. I sat down and had Jane try on about a dozen dresses— summer dresses—that she has hanging in the closet but hasn't worn. Well, we picked out six golf outfits that she can get into (things are fitting a little more snugly now) and look good on her. And there are about seven dresses that are excellent, the right length, that aren't too snug, that we will be taking along. We discovered another evening dress that I didn't know she had, and we'll take that along with the others that she has. Sometime this weekend we should go out and buy shoes. I frankly don't know where to go to get good ones—and I'll carry along a pair of the kind she bought some time ago because that will give me some idea of quality.

My hardest problems involve coping with what she conceives of as her responsibilities. She incessantly asks partial questions involving the house, involving people, involving appointments weeks in advance. I simply do not know what she's talking about or how to answer—and I try to answer in some way that will satisfy her. Most of her questions are now skewed. That is, they involve people we don't know or imaginary people. They involve things about the house that are taken care of or appointments that are taken care of.

There are times when she's downright nasty about Bronwyn, claiming that Bronwyn says bad things to her, or tries to "push" her into doing things she doesn't want to do, and remarking on the fact that Bronwyn doesn't say "hello" to her or ask her how she is, and so on.

Jane is becoming more and more insistent that I be with her all the time, even when going to bed. Jane will want to go to bed early—and I will want to stay up and watch something on TV or read. And she will be downright angry, will go up and get undressed, come down, go back up rather flouncing as she can do, then come back down, and so on. Sometimes her expression is rather wild, as if she doesn't know where she is.

My next hardest problems are getting Jane to do those things that she should do, or that are good for her—and doing things the same way each time. There are times when I ask her to do something and explain why, and she doesn't for some reason want to. She will rebel, really, or simply not do it. And now she is forever doing things so differently each day that I simply do not know what she is going to do. Her car keys are a token of independence and freedom for her, so it becomes important for her to carry them, which pleases me. But one day she'll keep them in the cupboard, another day in the Kleenex box, another day in a drawer, another day in her coat pocket—all the time her brain trying to figure out what is the best way to do things. She likes to go through the mail before I see it, which I also like her to do—but she distributes it to herself, to me, and so on without rhyme or reason, and sometimes I have to go look for important pieces that she has misplaced.

Jane doesn't really read anymore, and I guess this discourages me about as much as anything. She will sit in front of a paper, leafing through the pages without her glasses on. I know, of course, she can't see to read without her glasses. From time to time when I'm there and notice, I'll suggest she put on her glasses. Sometimes she resents this—but when she does put them on, she reads what is there and exclaims as if she's making a discovery. But she reads less and less, comprehends less and less, and really doesn't understand words anymore.

The neurologist was surprised and pleased that she still recognizes me, who I am, and so on. But I guess he expects that this will pass soon.

Jane likes to help me with the washing, and I like her to do this. But some of the things she does don't make sense. The other day, the washer filled with socks finished its cycle, and she removed the damp socks from the machine. Instead of putting them in the dryer, however, she paired the socks and tied them into pairs as if they were ready to put away in drawers.

She tries. She tries so hard, every thought being to be helpful to me, to be helpful to all of you. I don't think she's had a selfish bone in her body. But her trying, now, is an increasingly hard thing to handle.

One of the things that disturbs me is that I cannot at all times be gentle and calm with her. There are times, after she has incessantly said something or done something, that I speak sharply to her—not in anger, necessarily, although I think she thinks it's anger. And it hurts her and makes her weep, and then my heart just breaks. I keep telling myself never, never, never to speak sharply to her, and most of the time I manage not to be sharp with her. But as I say, there are times—less and less frequent, I believe—when I do speak sharply.

One of the qualities in her that enabled her to do so well in school, so well in college, so well at ETS and so marvelously well as mother and wife, is her quiet determination, discipline, and even stubbornness. I love and admire these qualities, even though now they present all kinds of problems. I am now explaining to her that when I'm away from home I want to have someone there to stay with her. But she still doesn't accept this, resists it, comments on Bronwyn. I continue to insist, however, because after this project is over I still will have to go into New York from time to time, or go someplace else, and I will want to have someone from the Princeton Homemaker Society come stay with her—even overnight when I have to go to Chicago on SOCAP or BAC business. But when she's made up her mind about something it takes a great deal of discussion and persistence to change her.

During the next six months to a year it's going to be most important—when you all call on the telephone—to talk with her about yourselves and, when she wants to hand the phone to me knowing you want to talk with me, for you to ask her to "get on the other phone," or say "Mom, stay on the phone so we can talk to you, too." It won't be long before she won't be able to understand. . . .

I don't mean to depress you; I really don't. At the same time I think you ought to know how she is and what's happening, and what's likely to happen. Keeping her clean is a real chore, for she doesn't like to take showers, she squirrels her dirty clothes away in drawers, she is dressing erratically—although she likes to dress up and look nice.

In some ways I think I should have kept a diary to keep track of her condition. And then again, what would be the purpose?

I am deeply glad that this hasn't been something like cancer. She enjoys life, and I love to see her enjoy it. I'm not sure she can really play golf again, because each time she addresses the ball now she does it in a different way—yet she likes the idea of playing and going with me. But I will begin taking her out with me when I play—in an electric cart—and she will just watch. We'll see how that goes at The Breakers. Something like this will have to be worked out, for I can't leave her alone now, and her friends don't really want to have the responsibility.

Because Harold thought Jane would like to see *Tootsie*, I took her to see it the other night. It was entirely different from *The Verdict*. At *Tootsie*, she laughed a few times—but generally thought it was "awful," and from time to time asked if it weren't time for us to go home. At *The Verdict*, as I told you, she felt the mood, the conflicts, the triumph, and so on—and came away saying she enjoyed it and it was "wonderfu." At the same time she says now that she enjoyed *Tootsie*. Simply because of the setting, the big screen, the concentration of so many people, she seems to comprehend movies better than TV shows, although she enjoys the simple shows, the soaps and "Love Boat," and Merv and so on. She seemed to like *Gandhi* (sp?) or *Ghandi* (sp), however the hell you spell it.

Alan, it tickles me that you are now advising Jun on

how to be a good salesman. And you *will* be of help to him. Guy, a high school classmate of mine in Nebraska wrote me and said she had heard on the CBS morning TV news a few weeks ago a "Guy Wirsig" from Los Angeles, and she wondered if it were my brother or some distant relative. I told her you'd be delighted to know you were on network—and that you were my son. And brother Paul, I'm glad the sale of Heller leaves things unchanged for some time and probably will work out for the best. Mom, by this time you may have decided what to do about the cataract operation—but if it's a matter of your being able to see better, I should think you would want to do it as soon as possible and not wait until just before you take your driver's license examination. However, if you have any doubts about the cataract operation and, deep down, don't want it, then by all means don't go through with it. You will make the right decision for you, I know.

Do be careful. Give Marilynne and Linda and Marcia and all the kids our love. Call us collect frequently.

Love,
Dad

7

Surgery at Dartmouth-Hitchcock — An Answer?

I kept searching for help. One part of me insisted that somehow, somewhere, there was an answer. Another part of me knew that there was no hope.

Still, I read and listened and still hoped . . .

One Wednesday afternoon, not long after my Naloxone fiasco and following the old-timers' golf at Springdale, my good friend William Wilson, former head of public relations for a major financial institution, casually asked me:

"Woody. Did you see on TV what the Dartmouth-Hitchcock clinic is doing about Alzheimer's?"

"No," I said, almost uninterested. People were always coming up to me to talk about something old, something tried and found useless, something I'd already read of or seen. They wanted to be kind and helpful, though, so after a while I welcomed what they had to say even if I already knew it.

"You'll be interested," Bill persisted. I waited—and he went on. "I heard about this new technique," he said. "And when I was visiting Dartmouth last weekend I went around to see them. Nobody was available except someone in public relations. But he gave me the whole story."

Still, I waited, saying nothing—but listening.

"This man—I have his name at home—said that the neurosurgery and neurology departments had performed an operation. What they did was this: They entered a· chemical directly into the brains of Alzheimer's patients. And the result were exciting. I asked for all the information he could give me—how someone would apply for the treatment, how long it would take, and so on. You might want to investigate . . ."

By this time my heart was pounding. Again, hope surged through me. It immediately sounded reasonable to me. Maybe it was the best theory yet. From my reading I knew that one of the serious problems facing Alzheimer's victims is that the chemical neurotransmitter acetylcholine seems to be missing in their brains. Researchers have wanted to replace the acetylcholine, but nothing passes the blood-brain barrier—at least when given orally or by injection.

Now, if someone found a way to infuse a chemical directly into the brain, a chemical that could replace the neurotransmitter acetylcholine, perhaps . . . perhaps it might do some good. Perhaps it could be similar to the help Parkinson's patients get from L-dopa.

My spirits soared higher than they had in some years. I hurried to Bill's home and got his notes and the names of people at the Dartmouth-Hitchcock clinic.

Bill had some further thoughts. "Apparently there was an article in the medical publication *Neurology* that describes what has been done. It was that article that brought the TV crews to Dartmouth. Watch TV tonight—it may be on some of the news programs."

That evening I devoured the TV new shows. Sure

enough, on one of the network shows was a segment devoted to the Dartmouth-Hitchcock project.

I watched in turmoil. I saw a gray-haired woman, said to be sixty-four—just about Jane's age, but looking years older than Jane—answer questions and talk about her illness. Before her treatment, the announcer said, she had been unable to talk—or walk. She couldn't recognize her friends or relatives. She could not cook or do anything else around the house.

Now, though, she talked well. She said she was enjoying seeing her friends "again" and visiting with them. Her pride that she could now get back into the kitchen to cook meals was obvious.

As she talked, her husband looked on, beaming with happiness. "She seems just like she used to be," he said.

By quick turns I was excited and depressed. "I've got to get Jane into that program," I kept saying to myself. Then I'd think, "But what if it doesn't work for her?"

I knew what it would take to get Jane in: letters from her physicians, from her neurologists, a letter from me describing the entire course of the disease as I remembered it. . . . We'd probably have to move to Hanover, New Hampshire, and live there, I thought. But that was all right. We could do that. It was little enough. . . .

First, I got hold of a copy of *Neurology*. Then I called the Dartmouth-Hitchcock clinic to try to speak to the director of public relations.

Many others had been calling, too. Once I got through I talked to a kind, helpful young woman who said she was sure she could respond to my questions. In detail, she explained what I should do to apply. She was not encouraging, I noticed, but she was professional.

The possibilities aroused enthusiasm in Jane's physician, Dr. Fulmer. It made sense to him, too. He said he'd be glad to write a letter of recommendation, which he did immediately.

Then I drove in to see Dr. Leon Thal, Jane's neurologist.

His response surprised me. I found his attitude was proper—but he was less than enthusiastic.

"You should know," Dr. Thal said calmly, "that this operation is quite invasive. As far as I can tell, the results are not much at all. Jane is pretty far along, you know. You may want to give this some second thoughts. . . ."

Stunned at this, I sat for a few moments in silence, Then, as calmly as I could, I said, "I've thought it through. It seems to be the best chance we've had thus far. I know Jane would be willing to take the chance if she could make a judgment. I—I'd appreciate your writing a letter."

When the letter came I felt disappointed. At first, I couldn't put my finger on why I was so disappointed. Then I realized that what he'd written was precisely accurate and factual, but it was such an overwhelmingly factual recitation of Jane's problems that the total impact seemed to be negative. His letter requested consideration—and that was all. At no point was he enthusiastic, or impassioned, or, well, persuasive.

What else might help? Sometimes, I thought, "professional courtesy" was useful. Since Jane's brother, Jim, was a distinguished professor of roentgenology at Boston General Hospital and Tufts School of Medicine, I asked him if he would write a letter. Through the years, brother and sister had not been close. But Jim was eager to cooperate in every way he could. He wrote a persuasive letter, one with dignity, that asked for major consideration for his sister.

What Dartmouth-Hitchcock was doing made good sense to me. I just had to get Jane in. For years, researchers had been trying to get a chemical past the blood-brain barrier and into the brain to act as a neurotransmitter in place of the missing acetylcholine. Nothing discovered thus far would pass that almost impenetrable barrier.

The neurosurgeons at Dartmouth-Hitchcock had decided to try implanting a pump in the abdomen, then to run a tube inside the body up to the skull. The next step was to bore a hole in the skull. Through the pump and tube, they would introduce a chemical directly into the brain.

The neurosurgeons and neurologists had suffused the brains of four patients with the chemical. Of the four patients, two had improved a great deal. One stayed about the same. And one seemed to regress.

My hopes were running high. "My God," I thought. "How wonderful. Even if Jane could only hold her own, stay the same, how great! How truly wonderful that would be! If only we can give Jane some time back in—well, back in her healthy life."

With all the persuasion I could develop, in my own letter applying for Jane, I described her career, how much she enjoyed being a wife and mother, how well she was—and how worthwhile it would be to arrest the disease. I explained that we could easily move to Hanover to follow whatever schedule was appropriate.

I did everything, in fact, that I thought possible. But I was worried, too. What if the whole operation really was too invasive? She couldn't stand much pain. And I couldn't bear to have her suffer.

Then I made up my mind: We'd go for it. We could handle the pain. The neurosurgeons would cope with the invasive problems of the operation. Again, I felt sure Jane would want to do it—to think again, to respond, to enjoy her mind, her family, her friends, her feelings. So I plunged ahead and sent the letter.

I remember vividly the day I received the answer from Dartmouth-Hitchcock. It was bright, sunny, cool, but warm enough to take Jane for a walk down Princeton's Nassau Street to look in the store windows.

When I saw the return address of the Dartmouth-Hitchcock clinic, my heart began to pound. With different feelings tumbling over me—excitement, anticipation, some dread, always the possibilities—I opened the letter.

Rejected!

There it was, explained in kindly words: The doctor was sure Jane was too far along to benefit from such an experimental procedure. That, I found, was hard to accept. But went on. There had been so many requests from everywhere, he said, that they had decided to limit those they accepted for treatment to patients within their immediate service area.

I was crushed. I felt that the last best hope for Jane was gone.

Had I done enough? The questions and self-recriminations began to pile up inside me. Perhaps I hadn't tried hard enough. Perhaps I should have gone up to Dartmouth and talked directly with the surgeons. Perhaps I should have tried to bring some pressure to bear on the decision. Could I have mounted an irresistible campaign to force Jane into the program? Should I have done that, even though the hospital staff might have been angry at my ramming something down their throats? The agony has stayed with me.

A year later I applied to Dartmouth-Hitchcock again, for I'd learned that they were now treating some fifty patients. Again I was turned down, for the same reasons. By this time I was angry . . . and torn. Was it really worth it to pressure for such an invasive technique? To chance it? Was it worth her suffering?

I did get some indirect feedback about the experiment. During a reunion of retirees at ETS, I met an executive who had worked with Jane but whom I had not met—at least, I didn't remember him. He seemed familiar with Jane's situation and chatted with me about Dartmouth-Hitchcock.

"I have a friend whose wife has gone through the procedure," he said. "The results have been inconclusive. That is, there hasn't been any what you would call 'improvement.' But—"and he emphasized his words, "he did say that she hadn't seemed to get any worse. The inevitable decline seemed to have stopped."

I swore under my breath. That, alone, would have been

a godsend. Just to keep Jane from declining further—just to let her keep on enjoying beauty, exclaiming over babies in strollers, violets growing beside the sidewalks. . . .

Early in her illness, Jane would leave sentences half-spoken.

"What, darling?" I'd ask.

She couldn't repeat what she had said. Nor could she seem to remember, or get out of her mouth, what she wanted to say.

She more and more frequently used incorrect words. At first, they came close to what she meant. Then, as the years went on, the words she used for what she meant were meaningless.

Yet from the beginning up to this very moment, Jane looks as if she knows—inside her head—what it is she's saying or trying to say. So many other Alzheimer's victims who have progressed as Jane has look wild-eyed, strange. They seem frantic or disturbed.

But not Jane. After these many years, she looks serene, calm, collected. She acts and behaves normally, as if she's completely aware of all that goes on about her, keeping it in perspective.

At times Jane will ask me a question in a way that tears at my heart. We will be sitting together and Jane, with that lovely and knowing smile, will grasp my hand, look deep into my eyes, and softly, so persuasively, ask me a question—nodding seriously to emphasize a point she's making. And her words are incoherent and incomprehensible to me.

She immediately senses that I don't understand her. Yet she yearns to have me understand. The appeal in her eyes is agonizing to bear. At times like these I think she must know exactly what she's saying—and must be frantic that I cannot understand. She doesn't, however, *act* frantic. When she senses that I don't understand, or sees that I am not responding as she wants, she simply sighs and turns away, a disappointed look on her face.

At other times, Jane will take my hand, hold it close to her, and again look deep into my eyes. Then, in her soft voice, as persuasively as she can, she will start explaining something to me. I interpret it to be what she wants me to do, or to do with her, or . . . or . . . or what? I never know.

At first, when Jane would talk to me this way, I would respond as softly and earnestly as I could, saying that I was sorry I couldn't understand. I'd ask her to repeat what she said. Each time I'd see the disappointment in her eyes, or the confusion. She would turn away from me for a moment, not angry, just baffled, confused, undecided.

Later, I began to try to anticipate the kind of message she might be conveying to me. I would answer, "I think so. What do you think?"

That seemed to satisfy her to some extent.

At other times, I would say, "I don't know. What do you think? And she often would respond at once, with relief, saying, "I don't know, either."

So now I try never to say that I don't understand, for I think she must know what I'm saying, I try to respond in a way that will satisfy her, respond to the message she seems to be sending, to keep our conversation going.

It seems to be better.

Jane can spot a baby stroller at five hundred yards.

Instantly, she will utter a few of the phrases she can still speak clearly—"Oh, look at him," or, "Isn't he cute?" Always it's a boy baby. Is this because her own babies were boys? I don't know.

Watching Jane look at babies is a lovely experience. She breaks into a benign smile. Her eyes literally shine with joy.

If she's close enough, while we're walking on Nassau Street, Jane will bend over, smile down at the baby, and utter her own incoherent sounds—always in a reassuring tone of voice.

Every time, the baby looks back at her and breaks into a smile, often gurgling at her voice.

When she's ready to move on with me, Jane will utter a reassuring phrase, such as, "You're a good boy," or "I'll see you soon again.

At these words, my heart leaps. Again I wonder if these rational, loving, so on-target thoughts come from her damaged brain cells. Or do they come from other parts of the brain? Are they mostly reflexive? They seem so coherent, so right for the moment and time, so thoughtful in every important way and so much like Jane in her best moments, that I do believe she knows exactly how she feels and what she's saying.

Some mothers enjoy Jane's obvious pleasure and admiration of their babies. They stop and smile proudly as Jane bends over their babies to coo and exchange gurgles.

Other young mothers are, well, different. It's understandable, but sad. These mothers become startled and upset by Jane's incoherence. They hurriedly push their carts away, passing Jane by as quickly as they can.

No matter how they treat Jane, her sweet, loving nature shows through. If a mother hurries by, Jane smiles down at the baby and waves good-bye, then moves on with me, a smile remaining on her lips and in her eyes.

In recent months, at the community church, a preschool child-care center has been set up. What a joy to Jane! She adores going past the playrooms. She smiles, and tries to banter with the aides as she used to josh with her friends. Jane watches the young mothers arrive with little four- and five-year-old children. As the youngsters race around her, yelling and pulling hair and tugging at each other, Jane beams down at them, surely in her element.

Jane could happily sit and watch groups of babies or little children all day.

8

The Promise of a Mind-Pill

My hopes rose again when I read in *Fortune* about the work of three drug companies that were researching a "mind-pill." It didn't surprise me, for it made sense to develop a drug, a "mind-pill," to protect the mind. Sometime, somewhere, research will come up with something that will bring help to Alzheimer's victims.

By this time after my rejection at Dartmouth-Hitchcock I was no longer afraid of another disappointment. The chances of finding some help for Jane were too important to worry about how I felt each time hope was dashed. I pushed into the job of finding out how far along these drug companies were—and whether I could enter Jane into their research programs.

Two of the companies weren't far enough along even to be willing to talk about it. But Warner-Lambert was already in the process of testing its mind-pill, I was told.

Now, how to reach the right people? I remembered that several years ago I'd met with the vice president of public relations at Warner-Lambert, Ron Zier. I like him. He had invited me around to talk about our consumer affairs, customer service audit—and was genuinely interested. At the time, he'd also tried to get me more interested in the hospice program Warner-Lambert was sponsoring. We had hit it off. He was soft-spoken, thoughtful, the kind of person who would respond to me.

When I called his office I found he was out of the country. One of his assistants told me how to contact the scientist in charge of the project directly.

Instead of telephoning, I wrote letters. If possible I try not to make a first contact by telephone. I'm reluctant, I guess, to try to be persuasive over the telephone when talking with someone the first time. I don't like people to do it to me.

In my letters, I reviewed Jane's history—and asked simply to have her accepted as a volunteer to try the "mind-pill" along with those who already were in the experimental group.

I know about double-blind studies, of course. I knew that we couldn't be sure she'd receive the pill; perhaps she'd get a placebo instead. But if the mind-pill worked on some people, it was likely that Jane would eventually receive the real thing—and earlier than she if she had to wait for it to be approved by the Food and Drug Administration.

The response was simple and straightforward. The scientist told me that their pill didn't really do very much for Alzheimer's victims. They were moving in the direction of using the pill for other illnesses. Besides, he wrote, Jane would have to be part of a control group at an authorized hospital or clinic—and they had no plans to expand their research program to include any other facilities. And so on and on. . . .

Rejected—again!

Well, not rejected so much as simply told that the pill didn't really work. There was no place for Jane to go.

I would have been glad to try to organize such a group

at Albert Einstein—if the word about the mind-pill had been at all encouraging. But even Warner-Lambert couldn't push it for Alzheimer's. At the time, there were no experiments being conducted among Alzheimer's victims. And there were no plans to carry on further experiments.

So nothing has worked thus far: not the Praxilene, not the Naloxone, not the mind-pill. It was hard not to give up.

Again and again, as I watch it happen, I marvel. As we walk, I suddenly see Jane become aware of a scene in front of her. She stops and exclaims, "Isn't it beautiful?"

To me, all the days of caring for her, the worrying, the stress—everything is worth it to hear her recognize beauty and utter one of her few phrases.

Last summer, while we were walking along Witherspoon Street, past the white-painted church, Jane suddenly became aware of the flower garden, the white picket fence, and the landscaping toward the rear of the church. She stopped and smiled.

"Now," she said, with a little wave of her arm, ."I like that!"

Perhaps it seems more extraordinary to me because most of the time Jane is so incoherent, so unable to express herself. Yet at those times when she sees beauty, the right phrase always seems to burst out of her.

As the months go on, however, she seems less and less aware of beauty. Sadly, it seems as if some beauty itself is passing away. . . .

One of Jane's most pleasant memories as a healthy young woman, when I met her, was her own grandmother, whom she called Nana.

So it seemed inevitable that when Jane became a grandmother she wanted to be called Nana.

Among all the sadness and regrets I have, one of the saddest is knowing that Jane has never really known her grandchildren. She has not been able to babysit for them, or even be aware of their growth.

While she was well, and even during the early days of her illness, Jane enjoyed shopping for Christmas presents for the children—and later, the grandchildren. She wrapped each present carefully, with love in every motion, then got them all into the mail with joy—and on time.

Our sons, knowing how much she likes being called Nana make sure that birthday, Mother's Day, and Christmas cards all address her as Nana.

Even today, as I read cards to her, Jane will smile and nod as I emphasize the words, "Dear Nana."

I drove Jane out to Cleveland a few years ago for the wedding of a niece. It was like an expedition into the Arctic—but I think Jane enjoyed it.

At first, the prospect of the trip seemed easy. I could take her to the men's rooms of gas stations, or rest areas along the superhighways, to change her Attends. Eating would be simple: everything except diner could be in the car. And we'd make the trip in one day.

What I didn't figure on was the cold, blustery wind that would whip at Jane as she walked from our car to the rest rooms.

Hating wind of any kind, anytime, I cursed the cold blasts as I helped Jane out ot the warm car, bundled her hood and parka jacket around her, slipped on her gloves, grabbed her red bag with the Attends and clothing changes in it, and plodded toward the men's room.

Usually, I had a choice of using the women's rest room or the men's room. At first, knowing that women were much more realistic and down-to-earth about bodily functions and sex than men are, I decided it would be easier to change Jane in the women's room. But I soon realized that all women didn't think alike. While they might be sympathetic to Jane, they didn't particularly like having me in their midst.

So I decided to use the men's room. If any man so much as dared to raise an eyebrow I'd clobber him fast, I thought. At least I would glare at him fiercely. There was no trouble with the men. And Jane couldn't have cared less.

The wedding was even more pleasant for Jane than I thought it would be. Another niece, married and with a two-and-a-half-year-old son, also attended. Jane had eyes only for the little boy. Her eyes feasted on him from beginning to end. As he toddled back and forth from one parent to the other, messing up his clothes with food and ice cream, suddenly squatting to inspect a shoe, Jane's eyes followed him, a lovely smile in her eyes and her soft voice repeating over and over again, "Isn't he cute!"

Getting Jane to bed was an elaborate routine.

First, there was the struggle with her teeth. She cannot brush them herself. But she doesn't want me to brush them, either. Yet I must. So I wheedle, speak softly, murmuring the one word that seems to work—"slowly, slowly"—and eventually she lets me get the toothbrush into her mouth. From then on it seems to work, especially brushing up and down. Sideways she likes least to all.

Sometimes, when I least expect it, she will take hold of the brush after I have it in her mouth and brush her teeth with all the old vigor and ability.

After brushing, I'll give her a mouthful of water—saying "now rinse, now spit it out." Usually she sloshes it around in her mouth and spits it out. At times, she swallows it, I've ceased to worry, knowing that the soapy toothpaste probably won't hurt her.

Removing her bridge so I can clean underneath it also is

a production. And I don't blame her for resisting. Because the spring is secure against two lower teeth, it must feel as if her mouth is coming apart when I release it. Taking my thumbnail and pressing it against one tooth at a time surely is uncomfortable. And she lets me know it in no uncertain terms. Still, I persist. Lately, I've begun to back her up against a wall so she can't move backward as I press the bridge out of her mouth. Finally, with a slight whimper, she lets me slip the bridge out.

Getting the bridge back in is another production. She simply does not like anyone messing around with her mouth. I don't blame her. But still, the bridge has to go back in. After I say softly again and again, "slowly, slowly darling," she will open her mouth and let me slip it in. When she closes her mouth and feels the bridge snap into place, a look of perplexed satisfaction comes over her face. It's the quizzical look I've come to enjoy through the years.

Then I toilet her, clean and wipe her. As usual, little things can make the sadness well up in me. If Jane should have a bowel movement before going to bed, I notice that she will reel off some toilet paper and fold it—as she once did when she was well. It would be the same length and be folded correctly—but then she wouldn't know what else to do with it.

Each time I oiled her, I was aware of how young her figure was, how smooth her skin . . . and of how much I loved her and had loved making love to her. Now, though, she was more like a young daughter to me.

Then to bed. In the motel where we stayed I led her to her bed, always on my left. I showed her where to sit down so she would be in the right spot to lie down. To her, this was pleasurable—yet typically she would utter a half-laughing, half-protesting babble of words as she lay down. Then I'd bring the covers under her chin—and look down into her eyes as she smiled up at me. And my heart would melt—again.

I'd kiss her again and again, wondering when would be the last time, I longing for such moments to go on forever.

"Why," I sometimes asked myself, "can't we believe in an afterlife as so many others do, that we'll see each other again . . . be together for all time?"

During the middle of our first night on the road, I awakened to see Jane half out of her bed. She was stretching toward me and the nightstand between our beds.

"Darling!" I called out, jumping up to keep her from falling. I changed her, fixed her pads and mattress protector, and tucked her back into bed. This time, I moved the bed up against mine so she couldn't possibly fall out.

Waking up in the morning with Jane was always a pleasure. I would see her watching me, peering over the tops of her covers, smiling, so knowing and filled with love. Her mind always seemed to work better early in the mornings.

"I love you," she would say, reaching out a hand to take mine.

"I love you," she would say again and again.

I would lean over and give her big kisses—and then I'd get her up to face the day.

That wedding trip will always be memorable to me—not because of any memorable event, but just because we were able to do it. I was amazed at the things we could do. All it took was the desire to try.

9

We're on TV — Innovations

As Jane and I sat in his office chatting one day in 1984, Dr. Leon Thal asked if we would be willing to participate in a TV project.

"Mr. Wirsig," he began, halting and not sure how to proceed, "do you think you and Mrs. Wirsig would be willing to—ah—be on a TV program about—about Alzheimer's?"

He hurried on, before I could answer. "Perhaps you'd rather not do—"

"Yes," I said. "If we can be helpful."

Why not, I thought!

He smiled and nodded, obviously relieved. "I don't know too much about it," he went on, "so I'll have them get in touch with you directly. I assure you, however, that it will be in good taste and not be intrusive."

A day or so later, I received a call from a Mr. Mernit, the producer of "Innovations."

"Have you ever seen the show?" he asked. "It's on the public broadcasting system."

"Sorry," I said. "Haven't even heard about it. I guess I'm the plebeian type."

He did me the courtesy of chuckling a bit and went on. "It's a half-hour show devoted to some important aspect of science, medicine, or our culture. Funds for the show come from major drug companies as well as other corporations. It's shown on stations all over the nation."

"I'm sorry I've missed it," I said. "I've probably missed some good shows."

"I think so," he said pleasantly. "Anyway, I understand you and your wife are willing to participate in a program we're thinking of producing on Alzheimer's disease. Am I right?"

"Yes," I said. "I told Dr. Thal we'd be willing to do it."

"Good," he said. "I'd like to come out to your home and visit with you and Mrs. Wirsig. And I can tell you what sort of thing we have in mind."

He turned out to be a pleasant, quiet-spoken man, youthful, thoughtful, who knew his business. As we sat talking, I could see him appraising our living room and the entrance to our town house, searching for the better camera angles. He was kind and attentive to Jane, which also pleased me.

"We'll want to get some shots of you and Mrs. Wirsig walking along Nassau Street," he said, "and coming out of your house, perhaps going in—that sort of thing."

I nodded. I could understand why.

"Mostly, though," he went on, "we'd like to focus on you here inside your home—talking about your personal lives, how you feel. That sort of thing."

"Okay," I said.

"I'll ask you rather general questions, off camera. And you just take off and talk about the subject for as long as you have something to say."

"Okay," I said again. I'd been on TV talk shows many times.

First, we filmed a segment of the program in Dr. Thal's

office. He went through the motions of giving Jane an oral examination—asking the kinds of questions he might use on a patient to achieve a diagnosis.

Jane looked lovely, I thought. We'd had her hair done, softly waved, but she wore no makeup. I hadn't put makeup on anybody since my drama days in college, so I didn't have the confidence to try to put any makeup on her. Nor did they. We all just went ahead.

When Dr. Thal asked Jane his questions, she answered in a flat monotone:

"What is your name?" he asked.

"Jane," she said.

"What is your last name?"

She responded, "Jane."

"What are the names of your sons?"

"I don't know," she said, after a moment's hesitation.

"Where do you live, Jane?" he asked.

"I don't know," she said.

I sat beside her, watching, my heart simply breaking as she tried to answer his questions.

In Princeton, we walked toward the camera on Nassau Street, holding hands. Then they took shots of our walking away from the camera.

The rest of the time we were inside our home, sitting on the living-room couch. That is where we did most of our talking. As I answered questions, Jane's constant mumble as she fingered a sweater could be heard in the background.

I'll always remember my first sentence—and apparently they did, too. It was the opening sequence of the film:

"It just kills the brain. . . ." I said, and went on from there.

The first half of the show focused on Jane and me, representing a typical couple, one of whom was a victim of Alzheimer's. In the second half of the program, several scientists talked about what Alzheimer's is, what has been discovered, and what science hopes to find out in the near future.

The program continues to be shown throughout the country. Three years later, I happened to be visiting my brother, in Denver, when it was scheduled. I watched it again, with members of my family who hadn't seen it before. The first half of the film, about Jane and me, remained the same. But the second half had been changed to focus on more recent research discoveries about Alzheimer's.

A good idea, I thought. This way, they can update the film again and again, keeping it current with the newest information, and still maintain the personalized quality.

I'm glad we did it. Jane, in watching the film, never by the flicker of an eyelash indicated that she understood it or even recognized herself or me. But many of our friends saw it. They would be kind, of course, but all of them seemed so genuinely pleased that I do believe we were really helpful.

Not long ago the Princeton *Packet's* Pam Hersh called me about an interview.

"We're doing a special report on Alzheimer's disease," she said. "Somebody said you and your wife would be helpful—especially about the day-care center you helped organize."

"I just suggested it, is all," I said. "Several community groups picked up on it."

"Still, I'd like to talk with you," said Pam. "And the other spouses of patients, of course."

Believing that I would be one of a number interviewed, and probably not quoted much, I opened up to her.

To try to help her understand what it means to have a loved one go through the progressive deterioration of Alzheimer's, I talked about my feelings. Later, I worried about what I'd said—and the way she might treat me. But then, it was done—so I shrugged it off.

As it turned out, Pam devoted almost two full pages of the paper to the story and sidebars. At the top of the first page was a big photo of Jane and me as I was helping Jane into the Prince of Peace Lutheran Church south of Princeton Junction, where the day-care center held its Tuesday and Thursday meetings.

The photographer knew his business. He had caught us with tense faces that showed our underlying anxieties.

Friends tell me that Pam Hersh's story was a good one. Her lead, and much of the story, focused on Jane. As might be expected, she contrasted Jane's brilliant career with her helplessness now. Then she reported what we discussed in her interview with me.

She mentioned the stress of caring for Jane and then quoted me as saying, "She made me happy for over 40 years. It's the least I could do." Which of course doesn't begin to express how I feel about Jane or what I would do to care for her.

In a situation of this kind, as with "Innovations," there's always the conflict between wanting to be of help to others, if possible—and wanting to keep inner feelings private. In each of these cases, I decided to talk and participate. Whether it has been of any help to others I'll never know.

Taking Jane to her day-care center meetings each Tuesday and Thursday requires planning and much persistence.

It starts about six-thirty in the morning. I get up and shave. Then I help Jane out of bed and into the bathroom to sit on the toilet while I wrap up her wet diaper and bed pads. Next, I put on her shower cap and help her into the shower. I get in with her; any hope of doing it another way, without getting sopping wet, is a dream. I get her wet, then soap her all over, taking special care of her hips, thighs, and groin area. She knows my motions by heart, so if I should do anything different; or even hint at tickling her, she protests with noisy vigor.

I dry her in the shower, rubbing her body so that it glows, then put on her pink bathrobe and step out. Off comes the shower cap and I comb her hair. Dressing is simple: matching blouse and slacks, after putting on an Attends diaper and a brassiere. With shoes and socks, and usually a sweater, she's ready to go downstairs to breakfast. Only I'm not ready. So I sit her down in an easy chair in our bedroom to watch TV.

When I'm dressed, I give her a big kiss, and then a bunch of quick little kisses, murmuring "sweetheart" and "darling." Jane answers "Mommy, mommy, mommy" and kisses me back, as she always did. She says "Mommy," but I know she means "Woodrow" or "darling." Then we go down to have breakfast.

Breakfast is Jane's best meal. I fix her two soft-boiled eggs. Then I feed her bits of toast with orange marmalade. Finally, I give her two prunes, a banana, and as many mouthfuls of cereal as I can get her to take.

Milk Jane will drink constantly. Every morning she takes a big glass of skim milk.

By the time we've finished breakfast and I've washed her mouth, it's 8:40 or 8:45—already late. Traffic through Princeton is already horrendous. There was a time when stoplights, left-turners who stop traffic both ways, and trucks seemed to conspire to make us even later. Now, I've calmed down a little and accept what seems inevitable.

My reason for wanting to get Jane to her day-care center on time, or a little early, is that the aides and patients gather in the kitchen to talk and make the morning cocoa. When Jane arrives in time to join the group, she smiles and saunters into the kitchen with all the élan she used to have at ETS cocktail parties.

I particularly enjoy watching Jane the moment she

enters the church. Aides see her and immediately call out, "There's Jane. Hello, Jane darlin'. Come join us."

Jane smiles in return, touches them reassuringly, utters what in her own mind, I'm sure, is a joke—and goes off into the kitchen with them. Sometimes she remembers I'm there and will turn, smiling at me, as if expecting me to join her.

Lately, though, she blithely moves into the group without giving me a second thought.

Sometimes I wait and watch as they come out of the kitchen, arm in arm, and walk down the hall to their meeting room. In the years since the day-care center started, Jane walks progressively more slowly. Her strides have become shorter and shorter, almost mincing steps—but she is still sure-footed.

Whenever there's a step to climb, or a break in the sidewalk to step over, Jane ceases her mincing movement and boldly steps up and over.

As I walk with her, and feel her strength and sturdy attitude, even her eagerness to walk, I vow again to keep her walking and walking . . . as long as she possibly can.

10

Complications: A Heart Attack

At times I've asked myself a question I can—and can't—answer to suit me. That question is this: What causes stress for me in taking care of Jane?

First of all, I've never before been conscious of stress, although during problems at *Look*, at *Woman's Home Companion*, at the advertising business magazine *Printer's Ink*, and at the Better Business Bureau I experienced real stress. But I wasn't aware of it as stress.

With Jane, taking care of her from 1978 through May of 1984 never seemed stressful.

At the end of a day I'd be tired, of course. But I thought nothing about that. Taking good care of her was something I could do. I felt I was doing a good job. She seemed happy and as contented as possible.

To be sure, I cared for her twenty-four hours a day. I enjoyed being with her, loving her much as a new mother learns to love her new baby. And the fact that caring for Jane stopped my work with the Business Advocacy Center didn't bother me one bit. I proved to myself the consumer affairs/customer service audit was a vital process and could, or should, grow to be as routine and as big as an annual financial audit. To myself I repeated, again and again, and believed it: "I've had a very good life, with all the accomplishments I could want. I don't need any more prestige and influence. I've had it. So I'm content to retreat into my home with Jane."

But apparently feeding her, taking care of her incontinence, dressing her, getting her to her day-care center and hairdresser, taking her for walks, cooking, and washing all produced a subconscious stress that was eating away at me. Worst of all, probably, was the inexpressible sorrow at what was happening to my wonderful Jane.

Despite my reading about heart disease and cholesterol through the years, I had not realized that stress can contribute to the deposit of cholesterol inside the arteries, especially inside the heart.

There was also a genetic factor in my developing aorta stenosis, narrowing of the aorta artery, and some calcification of the valve. Apparently I also was developing ischemic heart disease.

Although I believed I ate a good diet, and exercised fairly regularly, and took appropriate vitamins and minerals, a heart attack was waiting to happen.

One Saturday evening, after walking the golf course pulling a cart and golf bag, I lifted a heavy, new TV set from my car and carried it into the upper story of my house. Usually, I get a neighbor to help me with such things. But I was impatient, and no neighbor was around.

At about 3 A.M. that night I was awakened with a feeling of tension in the middle of my chest. I didn't have the shooting pains, the crushing feeling, one is supposed to have in a heart attack. And within an hour or so, the feeling was gone.

I did not, thank goodness, play golf on Sunday, as I usually did. And I had something of the same feeling in my chest on Sunday evening. So early Monday I called my

New York physician and friend, Dr. Leonard Stone, who besides being a fine internist is an acknowledged heart specialist.

"Woody," he said, "you just might have had a heart attack."

I cursed myself. How could I have been so thoughtless—especially since I have the full care of Jane—to lift a TV set into the house that way?

"I think," he went on, "you should have an EKG right away."

"Okay," I said. "I'll drive into New York and you can—"

"No, no, no, no!" he said hurriedly. "I don't want you driving around in case you did have an attack. Isn't there someplace in Princeton where you can go?"

"Jane's physician could help me," I said.

"Good," said Dr. Stone. "Get in touch with him right away."

I called Dr. Fulmer's office. He came on the phone immediately and said to come to the emergency section of the Princeton hospital—right away.

I drove to the hospital, parked in the parking lot, and walked into the emergency room. There they gave me the EKG. Dr. Fulmer looked at the results and, since he had nothing to compare it with, he sent me home.

"Come in tomorrow morning for another EKG," he said.

The next morning I was there for the second EKG. And then I went home. Dr. Fulmer said later that he'd called Leonard and, together, they had gone over my EKGs . . . and both agreed on the result.

"Woody," Dr. Fulmer said, calling me at home, "I want you to go into the hospital—right away."

My first thought was for Jane. She was at her day-care center. And I was frantic. How could I get someone to take care of her on such short notice? What a stupid, stupid fool I was.

I spent the next three hours calling the nursing agencies, and found one that would provide round-the-clock care. I called our longtime friend Barbara Platten to ask if she'd pick up Jane, bring her home, and oversee the nurses who were scheduled to come at once. A nurse herself at one time, Barbie would do a good job of it.

"Woody," said Barbara urgently. "For God's sake, get to the hospital. I'll take care of Jane."

So I got back into my car and drove to the hospital. When I entered the emergency section you'd have thought I was in the direst emergency. I was quickly put on a mobile table and told they would undress me.

"Just stay quiet," they said, nurses and doctors hovering over me.

And then they took my blood pressure. By that time, my blood pressure had climbed to something like 175 over 100. And even I became alarmed at that. But then I decided to yield to anything they wanted to do.

After an X ray of my chest area, they trundled me up to the top-floor intensive-care unit. Soon Dr. Fulmer came in to talk.

"Woody," he said, "you did have a myocardial infarction."

"Bad?" I asked.

He smiled. "What is bad? It was in the back of the heart. If you had to have an attack, it's the best place to have it."

By this time I was feeling well, realizing that at no time had I really been feeling bad. There I lay, in the hospital bed, amazed that I was there at all, a nitroglycerin patch on my chest, with orders to stay in bed and not get out for any reason. But I did get out to go to the john.

A number of interns came around to examine me. I had more stethoscopes pushed at my chest, until I felt like a switchboard.

One young bearded man leaned over to tell me something sotto voce, as if it were confidential:

"If this were England," he said, "you'd never have been hospitalized with what happened to you."

In a way, that was reassuring—except that I realized it

might just be a gambit to allay my anxiety. But I accepted what he had to say at face value.

During the next eight days I did all the usual things: Got up, began to walk, then walked more. After the eight days Dr. Fulmer sent me home, asking me to be moderate in activity.

The hardest part of those days in the hospital was worrying about Jane. I wasn't supposed to use the telephone, but one was there by my bed—and I used it, often. As often as I could I talked to Jane, reassuring her over and over again that I'd be home soon to see her. She couldn't answer coherently, but I knew she recognized my voice and surely understood what I said.

I saw her as she returned home from the day-care center. A look of sadness and confusion was on her face as she walked in the door. Then she saw me. Her face lit up and she smiled, holding out her arms for me to hug her. And hold her, kissing her a multitude of times, saying over and over again how stupid I was, that I wouldn't leave her like that again.

Six weeks later, I took a treadmill test. The whole idea of a treadmill test so soon after a heart attack upset me. Asking someone to walk a treadmill, at increasing speeds, until—well, until what? Was I supposed to keel over from exhaustion?

I walked, and kept walking, easily keeping up with the speed of the treadmill. Naturally, I was worried. Would this give me another heart attack? The little slip of paper I signed said it was possible, and even death might result. Then why, for Christ's sake?

Finally, I'd had enough. I called out "stop." I could have gone on and on and on, I explained. But I was afraid. What did they want me to do—go on and on until I blacked out, until I had another heart attack? It seemed so damned stupid to me. Why couldn't they have told me at what point to stop?

Anyway, the doctors said I could now resume all normal

activity—except lifting big TV sets out of cars. They said they didn't want me to walk thirty-six holes of golf in hundred-degree weather. Eighteen holes at a time was all right.

At times, I was aware of how casual I was about my heart attack. Somehow, I even felt removed from it. I felt almost no fear, although I made sure to do everything I routinely could do to prevent another. I went to regular exercise sessions at the hospital's cardiac rehab center. Two young women sat behind a battery of monitors, while I, with a battery-powered transmitter hung around my chest, rode a stationary bicycle for six minutes, then pulled weights, then walked another six minutes on the treadmill, followed by more calisthenics, and finally spent six minutes on the rowing machine. They took my blood pressure before and after the sessions.

One day, while I was on the treadmill, the nurse suddenly said, in an urgent voice, "Woody, stop and get off." She seemed upset but was trying to control herself. I quickly stopped and got off. She didn't want to alarm me, but I could see she was troubled. All she would say is that "your heart was having an erratic rhythm. I'll talk it over with your doctors."

"Woody," said Dr. Fulmer after he examined me, "your blood pressure was high that day. Apparently, your blood pressure fluctuates. So I think it would be wise to take some medication."

That worried me. I felt that Dyazide, through the years, had affected Jane's mind. I wanted no part of medication that could give me Alzheimer's.

"Don't worry," said Dr. Fulmer. "I'll give you the least possible amount of the beta blocker Tenormin. Five milligrams each morning. It'll slow down your heartbeat—and level off your blood pressure."

"But what are its side effects?" I asked.

"It's water soluble," he said. "No problem with the brain."

The Tenormin did, indeed, slow down my heart. It was sixty beats a minute normally, which is slow—an athlete's heartbeat. The Tenormin slowed it down to forty-five beats a minute, which is the borderline of safety.

I felt no effects of the Tenormin except that I felt a bit washed out at the end of a day. As I would wash the dishes, after dinner, I'd have a tense feeling in my chest, which I simply ascribed to being tired. Perhaps it was angina, which I did nothing about even though I carried nitroglycerin. Well, it didn't behave as I'd heard angina behaved. I thought angina was sharp, crushing pains in the chest. These weren't pains at all, just a kind of tense feeling.

During the following year, while I continued to take care of Jane—it seems almost a litany to repeat changing diapers, washing clothes, taking her for walks, cooking meals, doing interminable errands—I kept up my exercises and felt good. But during an examination by Dave Fulmer, he decided to make a change.

"Woody, I think I'll change your medication," he said. "I'll give you a different beta blocker."

"Why?" I wanted to know.

"Well, the EKG showed that your pulse was lower than forty-four per minute. That's too slow."

"Umm," I murmured, waiting.

"I'll give you pindolol, five milligrams in the morning and five milligrams at night."

"Twice as much as Tenormin?"

"It's just different," Dr. Fulmer said. "It will let your heart beat at about fifty-one beats per minute. It'll be better."

The whole idea of taking a beta blocker for the rest of my life gave me the creeps anyway. The nurses at the rehab center kept saying that "if you're on a beta blocker it's not wise to push your heart too much in exercise."

"What about exercise?" I asked Dr. Fulmer and the cardiac specialist. "Here I am, supposed to exercise to keep a healthy heart, yet I take medication that stops me from exercising."

"You can exercise with the beta blocker," they said. "But not too much. On the bicycle, or walking, take your heart beat up to seventy a minute and hold it there for six or seven minutes."

"But it seems such a contradiction in terms," I protested.

"We just don't know any more about it," the doctors said.

At least, I thought, I can do something about my diet. I had been on a low-fat, low-cholesterol, low-salt diet—and Leonard Stone had clocked my cholesterol at 180, with the high-density lipoproteins at a good level and the low density lips at an appropriate level. So I applied even stricter standards. No fat, except that found in chicken, fish, and the best breads.

For breakfast I fixed a mixture of nonfat, high-fiber cereals; nonfat milk; two prunes; a banana; the whites only of two hard-boiled eggs (I put the yolks out for the birds); and Postum. Not even decaffeinated coffee!

For lunch: Some low-fat cottage cheese, nonfat yogurt, a glass of nonfat milk, one slice of high-fiber whole-wheat bread (3 grams of fat), and an apple.

For dinner: A salad of lettuce, endive, cucumber, and peppers, with a salad dressing of tomato juice spiced with a salt-free combination of spices; baked breast of chicken; a baked potato without anything on it; usually a mixture of broccoli, cauliflower, carrots, and zucchini squash; and for dessert a combination of frozen fruits, including peaches, grapes, blueberries, strawberries, and melon balls, defrosted in the microwave.

It was enough, I knew, to make a gourmand blanch!

Still, I felt that it might be possible even to reverse the heart disease. I'd read that Pritikin, with clogged arteries at the age of forty, put himself on essentially a fat-free diet. By the time he committed suicide at sixty-nine, he had clear arteries. Possibly it was cause and effect. If so, possibly it could work on me. I have since learned, however, that experts now believe that after the age of sixty-five the cholesterol is so calcified that no reversal is possible. Thwarted again! Still, I would try. . . .

11

Warts — Or a Probe of My Psyche?

"If you go on like this, Woody," my brother Alan said one day, "we're going to lose two good people instead of one."

My family, I realized, was concerned about me.

"We should talk, I think," Alan went on. I sensed an unusual note in his voice. Even though he was so like our father—quiet, strong, slow to anger—this was unlike him, for we often talked without any formal preamble. I waited.

Slowly, Alan spelled it out. "If you keep on working like this with Jane, the stress is going to get you. You'll die."

"You may be right," I said. "Of course I want to live—as much for Jane as for me. And I don't want to act in ways that will—well, end things too soon. I thought I was handling it well. But what else can I do? She needs me."

"Then taper off," Alan said, quite sternly for him. "If you have to, let some of her needs slide a bit. That's tough, I know. But it seems to me it's your only choice."

123

"I don't know—" I said, my thoughts going to that sweet-faced, dear woman, my wife, sitting in a chair, confident, it seemed to me, that I would be coming around soon to be with her. I couldn't find anyone to take care of her the right way. I know, for I kept trying.

"You act guilty," Alan went on, an impatient tone in his voice I'd never heard before. "Is there something behind all this? Something we don't know?"

For a moment I almost hated him. Guilty? How dare he! Yet as I plunged down into my innermost thoughts I realized—again—as I had so many times, that yes, I did feel guilty about some things. Perhaps I was trying—inevitably failing, but trying nevertheless—to make up for things I had done, or not done, for Jane during our forty-five years together. As I reflected, it wasn't so much things that I did or didn't do, for I loved her and never wanted to hurt her in any way. But in my selfishness, my thoughtlessness, there were actions I took—or didn't take—that could have made some of Jane's moments happier, freer of responsibility, that could have brought her closer to me.

As I think back, the list isn't very long. And it would seem ludicrous to couples who lacerated each other. But there was the time, for example, when we moved into our last home, the Princeton townhouse. We set up a breakfast table in one end of the kitchen. In our previous home, we had been eating our meals in front of the television set.

"Now," said Jane, a note of satisfaction in her voice, "we can eat dinner here—so we can talk."

My mind a million miles away, I mumbled that I wanted to keep on eating in front of the TV. At that, I did notice, Jane leaned back in her chair in the den, her eyes closed—in sadness, in pain, a kind of despair? Was I—were we—not talking much at home, now after work, when we were together? I will always remember that scene with sadness. How I wish that I could have understood her need—and given the little effort it would have taken to eat our dinners together in the kitchen . . . and talk.

There was a time Jane was doing our accounts—and, in retrospect, it must have been a year or two after she began showing evidence of her Alzheimer's, although I didn't know it at the time. Jane got up from her chair and came into the den, where I was reading a magazine, to ask me a question. Her lips were quivering as she asked me the question. I answered, perfunctorily, I'm sure, and turned back to my magazine. I did notice her pause for a moment, undecided, then go back to her chair. In a few moments, she was back, asking me the same question and nodding her head with emphasis. I answered her with some irritation, which she sensed. Her lips quivering again, she returned to her chair.

A few moments later, I got up from my chair and went out to her table and took her in my arms. I kissed her and held her tightly. "Darling, darling, sweetheart," I said. "I'm sorry. I didn't mean to be sharp. I want to help."

She began to weep and shook her head despairingly. And I noticed her worksheets—with numbers, additions, subtractions at random all over the papers.

"It's so hard," she said through her tears.

I held her and comforted her. Soon she was smiling and went back to her papers. I knew that she liked doing the accounts, liked the detail, liked the knowledge of how our lives worked that she could see through those figures. So I left her and went back to my magazine. Yet ever since, and especially now, I've felt remorse and wish so desperately I'd been kinder when I had the chance.

There were other things—small things, perhaps, but important—that would have meant so much to Jane. Shopping for our food, for example. I could have done this once or twice a week, easily, and it would have been a welcome respite for her, with so much else to do. Yet I'm sure she felt my three hours on the train into and out of New York each day took my time, so she willingly did the shopping. I might have given Jane more time to herself after dinner by clearing away the dishes and loading the dishwasher. I could have done that easily, rather quickly—and let Jane get to her newspaper sooner. Reading her paper in the evening was something she looked forward to all day. Sadly, just before she began to be ill, she would often fall asleep in the middle of her paper and never get through it. Whenever this happened, she would sigh as if somehow she had been defeated. Sometimes I would take care of those after-dinner dishes. But not regularly, and it wasn't something Jane could count on each evening. Uncomplainingly, she went ahead and cleaned up after dinner. And I buried myself in my reading.

"You seem to be 'up' all the time now, Woody," Alan said, still asking uncomfortable questions. "Don't you ever feel angry? Or frustrated? Or bitter at what life has dealt you and Jane?"

"Yeah, yeah," I answered quickly. Then I stopped to think. "I've said before," I went on, "that I'm too busy to cry. Yet somehow it seems to me that I'm almost crying all the time. Late at night, when I'm lying awake, unable to sleep, my heart aching for Jane, my chest gets tight. I can't breathe for the sorrow I feel. I think so often that I have no happy moments left in my life, except for those times when I'm walking with Jane or holding her hand. . . ."

"Possibly," Alan said firmly, "but—you enjoy golf now, don't you?"

"Yes."

"And you like watching baseball and football? You like tennis?"

"Yes," I said.

"Well, then. . . ."

I thought about several of his questions. Rage? Bitterness? I've never really thought—or talked—consciously about such feelings.

"Yes, I guess I do rage, at times," I said. "I rage against the fate that took Jane away from her work, is taking her away from her family and me. We could be doing so many things together. More traveling. More golf together. Seeing more theater, reading together more. A million things we could be doing together, especially if she had retired normally.

"And bitter? Of course I'm bitter . . . bitter that it's happening to us. Why? Why us?

"And yet, I—I think it's stupid to dwell on any of it," I went on. "What good is it to rage against something like this? Something I can't do anything about? It only makes me feel worse. So—I don't think about it much.

"Bitter? Well, think of how much worse it could be. What if Jane had cancer and suffered terrible pain for months, even years? What if she had broken her back in an accident and was a paraplegic for the rest of her life? What if—Dozens of things could be worse. Remember, I'm pretty sure she doesn't know what has happened to her. She may very well think everything is normal. I'm sure of it. In so many ways it's one of the least tragic tragedies to happen to an individual."

"But not the families," Alan muttered.

He thought for a few moments, then went on. "You've said many times that Jane is beloved by everybody. Everybody? You mean she never made an enemy? Never made someone mad? Nobody can be that perfect."

I said nothing for a while, thinking before answering. He was only trying to get me to talk it out, to release some of the stress he was sure was piling up inside me.

"No, not perfect," I said. "I never said she was perfect. Other people did. Jane would be the first to say 'not perfect.' I imagine she wishes she were less passive and more assertive. The poor girl was always trying to decide whether to get her crooked front teeth straightened. Her nose, she always thought, was much too big. Should she get it bobbed? To me she was beautiful just the way she was—and I told her so, many times. She always tried to do the best she could with what she had. And what she had was goddamned good.

"As for enemies? Well, I can think of at least one. Of

course she had to fire several people. And get tough with some suppliers. But there was one person at ETS who never felt Jane was beloved. After Jane took on Information Services, a hot-shot young writer type came to work. Wealthy, good-looking, with large breasts she thrust at any man who'd look, she was turned over to Jane to put to work. To use her 'abilities,' they said. For a while, things worked out well. She could write—but I still didn't trust her. She was very ambitious. Very ambitious. Jane, she felt, was holding her back. Behind Jane's back, she began sniping. She elbowed her way around the institution. Jane got wind of it but didn't know what to do. This was her first experience with such a person and she was baffled. To say the least, relations between the two cooled down to a freeze.

"Jane, instinctively or with wisdom, I never knew which, encouraged the hot-shot woman to try to work directly for some of the ETS top executives. This appealed to the hot-shot, of course. Soon she was transferred to the staff of one of the executives. She was out of Jane's hair.

"Later, the woman had the audacity to ask Jane to sponsor her for membership in a local golf club. Being vindictive myself, I was glad to see Jane turn her down."

Alan was listening, nodding his head. "You picture Jane as a lovely, almost angelic, sweet person. Perhaps that is true, generally. But aren't there some things about Jane you wish were different? Or that caused you to be sorry, or angry?

"What about the boys? You don't talk much about their visiting Jane. How do they react to her illness? Are they worried about themselves? About their families?

"Don't you have any resentment . . . any negative feelings?"

I didn't answer him, but I was thinking. Remembering. There was one period in Jane's illness when she went through a phase of anxiety—so much so that we had to give her mild sedatives. At times, Jane would become impatient with me. And she would vent her frustration.

While I was dressing her one day—getting on her panty hose was always a wrenching task—Jane wanted to sit down. I wanted her to stand for a few moments.

"No," she said, firmly.

"Yes," I said, just as firmly.

Suddenly, she hit me on the shoulder with her fist. With a straight face I tried hard not to laugh. She had softened the blow to a little tap, but must have thought she had belted me—Jane, who couldn't even slam a car door hard. The look of horror and remorse in her eyes let me know how she really felt. She didn't mean it, of course, and was sorry. I hugged and kissed her. And then finished putting on her panty hose.

As Jane's illness progressed, she would at times criticize something I did, or said—or didn't do. This, too, was a phase that lasted perhaps four or five months. One of those times, I remember, happened at The Breakers during our annual seniors' golf tournament. When she could play in the women's golf events, Jane enjoyed that outing as much as I did.

Among the most enjoyable activities, evening meals were "events" in The Breakers' huge, elegant dining rooms. On this particular evening, we arranged to have dinner with our Princeton friends, Audrey and Fred Short. Audrey, who ran her own real-estate agency, had been the first woman chairman of the Princeton Area Chamber of Commerce. She had encouraged Jane to be active in the Chamber. In her modest, steady way, feeling she should represent ETS in some community activities, Jane agreed to participate. Since Fred was one of my regular golf foursome at home, we all had much to talk about.

Before the conversation even began, Jane for some unknown reason seemed angry. Perhaps she thought we were going to ignore her and talk among ourselves. She began to complain, in words that tumbled out incoherently. And she kept on, and on. It was so unlike her I was shocked. I tried to calm her. I tried to get her to talk about our sons, or golf. But she wouldn't stop. Who knows what maelstrom of jumbled thoughts was coursing through her mind?

She kept on. She wouldn't stop. Even though Audrey and Fred were our good friends, and certainly understood the situation, I couldn't bear to see Jane so agonized. I smiled at her, stood up, and helped her stand up.

"Come on, darling," I said. "Let's go dance." As I left Audrey and Fred I said that we wouldn't be back. We'd probably dance a while and then go on to bed.

For years afterward that episode kept recurring to me. I always wondered what it was that troubled Jane. What was it that she wanted to communicate? I've speculated, of course. Perhaps she was venting some long-standing feeling. Maybe she thought she was excluded from conversations. Or felt she was ignored in such groups? Or felt I was slighting her—or—or—whatever. Through most of our years together, we communicated well, even by a glance, and our conversations were always on the same wavelength. As she began to be ill, however, Jane's questions sometimes became so skewed I couldn't answer them. Or she seemed passive, even uninterested in conversations, not listening. I know that I tended, whether with friends or with our sons, to direct my talk toward them instead of to her. At one point, she complained that we didn't "talk to her."

I never really knew, for sure, what set her off. But the memory haunts me and is part of my remorse.

"When you talk about Jane now," Alan went on, relentlessly it seemed to me, "you sound as if she's more like a little daughter to you."

"I guess so," I said. "She's so sweet. So helpless."

"Does that mean you no longer love her as a sweetheart—or a wife?"

An outrageous question, I thought. What does it matter

to anybody else? Yet I knew what he was after—wanting me to know myself, to understand what had happened and was happening to me, and above all to adjust to reality.

Of all that Jane and I have lost in her illness, one of the most wrenching is what has happened to our sexual lovemaking. It's almost impossible to talk about. Yet it's an integral part of us. Illness affects everything we do and think, even lovemaking.

If possible, it's even more of a tragedy because of the way we loved each other from the beginning.

After we realized we were in love at journalism school, we felt a total, exhilarating joy in our lovemaking. Although I'd had some experience with girls—indeed, was married—Jane came to our lovemaking with all the élan of an eager, unafraid virgin. She was an enthusiastic natural, and it enhanced every other quality I loved about her.

We were reckless in one way, letting our sense of triumph over mores act in a way that could have gotten us thrown us out of school and ruined our careers. Our school dean, Carl W. Ackerman, whom we liked, represented what we regarded as stuffy, old-fashioned attitudes about almost everything, including love. As I worked evenings on the Pulitzer Prize Committee duties, Jane came in to help. We decided that it would be appropriate, an appropriate flaunting of our feelings, to make love right on the dean's couch in his office. He'd faint, if he knew—so we imagined his knowing without the nuisance of his really knowing.

If we were caught we'd probably be expelled, of course. Our careers would be jeopardized. Yet Jane was just as enthusiastic as I was. It was compelling. It was exciting.

Throughout our married life we enjoyed our sexual relations. They became an integral part of expressing the love we had. Somehow, Jane and I found the right timing. She never, ever, refused me. I think I never proposed when she wasn't ready. We were not, and never wanted to be, sexual acrobats. We simply enjoyed each other, talking, caressing, endlessly talking.

When Jane began to be ill, although at the time I didn't realize what was happening, we both were experiencing some turmoil in our work. Neither of us realized how much the other was troubled. Nor did we talk much about it. It wasn't a deliberate choice, but because so much of our lives were untroubled we simply didn't talk much about such problems. In a way, I think each of us felt the other had his troubles under control.

After Jane's illness was diagnosed, and I began increasingly to care for her—especially bathing her and diapering her—we stopped making love. I loved her even more, if possible, but it was different. Whatever happened to our lovemaking was my doing. Certainly Jane did not refuse me. Perhaps she would have enjoyed it. But I could not. At the time, I was so busy, and so tired, I didn't analyze it. Maybe I had begun to feel that in her helplessness she was like a little child and I couldn't have the old feelings toward her. Perhaps I needed the stimulus of an active, participating mind to want to make love. Whatever the cause, making love became the farthest thing from my mind.

So very often I dream about Jane and the way we were. My dreams are pleasant, often filled with fun, usually gratifying. Even now, disabled as she is in her mind and rigid as her body often is, Jane might enjoy and even respond to lovemaking. Might, I say. But I would shrink from even trying. As I look at her sweet mouth, and cover it with kisses, her lips respond to mine. Her eyes beam at me, still so knowing. I realize, with a terrible aching loss, that, as with so many of the things we did and enjoyed, our lovemaking is over.

12

The Last Cruise

A part of my hope, of my search for help, was a desire to do things with her "before it was too late." I had no specific idea what "too late" would be, or when it would come. All I knew was that day by day, week by week, I wanted us to do—again—some of those things we'd always enjoyed.

I made up my mind to take Jane on another cruise. This one, I was sure, would be our last together. I wanted it to be a long cruise, on a good ship, to places we had never seen before.

Jane has always enjoyed shipboard life, and I've enjoyed watching her being happy. From the beginning of our cruising, when as editor of *Look* magazine I sailed with Jane on the shakedown cruise of the *Independence*—it was a winter week's sailing around Bermuda and back to New York—Jane has enjoyed the breakfasts, the day's lectures or reading in the library, dressing for dinner, deciding on the entrées, then dancing until bedtime. In between, there would be walks on the promenade deck to watch the interminable sea slip by—and at night, to wonder at the full moon hanging on the horizon like a lantern in a garden.

When our sons were in grade school, we took them on

an overland tour of Europe. A big part of the joy was sailing over on the *Queen Elizabeth* and sailing home on the
Queen Mary.

To me, the *Queen Mary* was familiar. A decade earlier,
I'd sailed with Captain Grattage, famous captain of the
ship, and enjoyed the small cocktail parties in his suite. A
large, ruddy, and imposing man, with a genial smile and
a charm the British seem to manufacture wholesale, Captain Grattage had a surefire way of encouraging his guests
to have another cocktail. "Of course," he would say, "we
must have the other half."

On that trip, Jane as usual was a master of time and
motion. She handled the boys' clothes, washing habits,
and eating so that the right things seemed to happen auto-
matically. As we toured just about every country in Europe
by bus that summer, there were no crises—except, perhaps, the day we visited the Colosseum in Rome and, in
mid-tour, Paul suddenly had to find a toilet. We located
one just in time.

A high point of that tour was being invited for cocktails
with Ava Gardner at her apartment near the Spanish Steps
in Rome. As usual, she also had several other friends—
and my family made it a crowd. Ava and her friends were
especially taken by our youngest, Paul, whose open and
innocent-looking face did not quite camouflage an intense,
inquiring mind. As we were leaving, Ava planted a big kiss
on Paul's cheek, which he of course refused to wash for
about a week afterward.

Several years later, Jane and I took the boys on a special
cruise from New York through the Mediterranean to the
Black Sea and back, a six-week odyssey that we will always
remember. At least the boys and I will remember it. It was
an experimental cruise organized by American Express—a
one-class cruise on the Atlantic, with 350 passengers,
among them perhaps 35 children.

Again, Jane was in her element. The food, the shipboard
activities, the shore excursions in Europe and Africa were

superb. Nothing went wrong—except for the last evening before landing back home. I had won a magnum of champagne for dancing with Jane, or hitting golf balls, or something. Anyway, I contributed the champagne to the young people. Our youngest, Paul, enthusiastically imbibed too much, a fourteen-year-old doing his best to act seventeen. Jane and I had gone to bed when Guy knocked on our cabin door. There, in his arms, was Paul hanging loose— and a bemused look on Guy's face.

"He's drunk," I said, and took him from Guy. My hold on him gave way and Paul slumped to the floor, as relaxed as a bunch of rubber bands and just as hard to hold. We put him to bed, where he slept through the night, and wakened the next morning unable to remember anything about the previous evening. He didn't even have a headache.

Several years ago, while Jane could still dress herself, walk well, generally remain continent, and participate in activities, I took her, along with my then ninety-three-year-old mother, on a fifteen-day cruise of western Europe and Russia. This was our first experience with the Royal Viking line. I decided these ships were what we wanted from then on. We fell in love with the ship—the *Royal Viking Sea*. Like its two sister ships, the same in every respect, the *Royal Viking Sea* was the cream of cruising liners.

Jane seemed to enjoy every moment—from the day we took off to fly to Copenhagen, where we were to pick up the ship, until we returned home. Again, it seemed a perfect time. The Baltic and North seas were calm—calm as mill ponds, literally. I can't remember the ship's tipping the least bit. Dancing each evening was like dancing on a ballroom floor at home. We enjoyed the shore excursions at Amsterdam, at Hamburg. We flew to Berlin, marveling at the busy, energetic flow of people in West Berlin and the drab, uninviting East Berlin.

I would talk with Jane about my feelings. She would listen but say nothing. I enjoyed being alone with her, yet I was sad, too, unable to communicate except by kisses, holding hands, hugs.

Quickly Jane decided she liked a special lounge high above the rest of the ship, where we could enjoy tea, cakes, and cookies while watching the sea.

By this time I'd decided we would not fly from Leningrad to Moscow. Instead, we spent all our time enjoying Leningrad—and were glad we did. My good friend, Kline Fulmer, who had been one of the first architects to visit Soviet Russia following the revolution, always spoke in awe of the beauty of Leningrad. I could see what he meant, of course; the city was laid out in such an orderly way, with wide streets and many open areas. But beauty? It wasn't my idea of beauty.

All her life my mother had been wanting to visit the huge Hermitage Museum, housing the world's largest collection of seventeenth and eighteenth century paintings—and she wasn't disappointed. Our tour lasted some five hours. This ninety-three-year-old was on her feet the whole time, while women half her age seemed to get the vapors and cried out for periodic rests.

Our guide sensed Jane's and my mother's differences and accommodated our tour to their speed.

Jane, in her way, and my mother and I admired Helsinki and its surroundings more than any other place during our trip. We visited a planned city as well as Eliel Saarinen's famous retreat, a woodland area, idyllic for creative communing with nature. Helsinki, we all agreed, was a place where we could all enjoy living—at least in summertime.

Jane and I especially felt comfortable in Copenhagen. True, we enjoyed Stockholm, but it was Copenhagen we liked best. We simply enjoyed walking, especially during our visit to the Tivoli Gardens. It seemed more mannered, controlled, less exuberant than many amusement parks I've seen around the world.

My mother's comment about Copenhagen made me

laugh. It was so typical of her—an ambivalence between the morality of her youth and the intensely modern woman she had become.

"Oh," said my mother, "I don't think I could possibly live in Copenhagen."

"Why not?" I asked.

"Why—the girls don't wear brassieres," she said.

With such memories, and many others in my mind, I wanted to plan a cruise for Jane and me that would be the best ever. By this time, however, Jane was walking more slowly, with shorter steps. Suddenly, she feared to sit down, to get up, to lie down in bed. All at once, it seemed, the logistics of taking care of her on such a cruise seemed overwhelming.

If anything, though, I was stubborn. I began to talk with Jane about where we might sail. By this time she could not respond to what for her were such complicated questions and ideas. I'd suggest a cruise to the Mediterranean and she would look at me questioningly, her eyes wide open, her mouth smiling, listening, her head cocked slightly. She seemingly wanted to understand but was frustrated by my words.

I made the decision myself. I decided we would sail in the wintertime to the New Zealand–Australia–South Pacific area. Several decades before, on my round-the-world trip for *Look*, I'd been to Singapore and Jakarta, but never closer to New Zealand and Australia.

In the back of my mind, for several months, was the thought of the *Royal Viking Sky*'s Round-the-World Cruise. Its Pacific segment was forty days from Los Angeles to Hong Kong. The ship would sail from Los Angeles on January 31 and arrive in Hong Kong around the middle of March, taking us into the summer of the southern hemisphere.

Whenever I mentioned the cruise to my family, or to friends, they would try to be encouraging—but look at me askance, as if I had taken leave of my senses. How could

I plan such a thing only a few months after my heart attack? My physicians didn't actually come right out and tell me not to go, but they seemed less than enchanted by the idea.

Still, I knew I could do it. Taking care of Jane on board ship, in our cabin, would be like taking care of her at home, and I wouldn't have to cook. All I needed was plenty of equipment, namely the disposable diapers. Above all, I thought Jane would enjoy such a cruise and might even benefit from it.

Instead of flying to Los Angeles and boarding the ship on the same day, Jane and I flew out a day in advance. I didn't like such close schedules. What if something went wrong? We'd miss the ship and miss the whole trip. And Jane, now that she was having more difficulty walking, perhaps would present troubles getting through traffic and the boarding routines.

But, as usual, she proved to be a trooper. Surprisingly, once again she was able to sit down. She could stand up and lie down without trouble. She seemed to understand the excitement and share in it. Guy drove us to the dock-side, where we walked up a broad stairway to the reception area. There a band played. Waiters circulated with trays of champagne. In her eagerness, Jane clasped my hand again and again.

That reception seemed interminable. Jane sat down near my mother, sister, aunt, and Guy. Our old friends Scotty Welch and Hu Pryor came to see us off and visit the ship. None of us drank anything. We simply waited. Finally, we were allowed to go on board. We found our cabin easily. Our first fears were over—our bags were already in our cabin. My second fear—where were the Attends diapers? The huge box was there, all right. I'd thought that if we must we could do without a change of clothing—but I absolutely had to have those diapers.

Cabins on luxury ocean liners are well-designed to conserve space while providing plenty of room for clothes. I discovered one whole closet I could devote to the diapers. I piled diapers in that closet from the floor halfway to the top. Above them I hung Jane's rubber pants. And we were set. We were ready for anything.

Our main objective—or, I should say, my main objective for Jane—was to enjoy shipboard life. The shore excursions, at Tahiti, Bora Bora, Tonga, New Zealand, Australia, Bali, Manila, and Hong Kong would be nice—if we could manage. But it was the ship itself we looked forward to, and it lived up to expectations.

Our stewardess, Mybrit, kept us stocked with apples and oranges and offered to bring us breakfast each morning. But I knew Jane would prefer to have our meals in the dining room, with all its ceremony and clinking glasses. As I'd asked, our table was for two and located in a corner with a view of one of the dining rooms and the ocean. One of my reasons for liking the Royal Viking line is that all eating was at one sitting only—so you didn't have to either eat in a hurry and too early, or eat into bedtime.

Our two waiters, Manuel and Marino, were tall, handsome, eager young men from Italy and Spain. Jane took to them as if they were two more sons. They, in turn, were careful and respectful of her, hovering over her, trying to understand her moods and her utterances. When she smiled, though, she won their hearts. Somehow she understood enough of their humor so that she enjoyed their work.

By this time I was feeding Jane at each meal. Dozens of tables in that dining room were in view of us. But, to my knowledge, nobody seemed upset at my feeding her. Everyone seemed instantly to understand. They responded to Jane's smile and her efforts to participate.

Each morning I made sure Jane had two soft-boiled eggs. Manuel and Marino each vied to fix the eggs, burning their fingers and probably cursing under their breath. But outwardly they were all smiles and care. As they placed the eggs in front of Jane, they would watch anxiously, wanting to get them just right for her. They had soft bran muffins ready, served cold cereal and milk, prunes, some orange juice, and decaffeinated coffee. We've rarely been waited on by anyone who seemed to care so much about the nice details of service. I knew their concern was genuine—and knew that I would tip them more than usual. The food was superb.

So our meals, as I'd hoped, became joyful experiences— even on those formal evenings when I would dress Jane in an evening gown. I'd brought along three of her evening gowns that I thought I could handle. I would switch from one to another so that she didn't appear in the same dress two evenings in a row.

I was pleased and sad at the same time that Jane seemed to enjoy wearing high heels—pleased that she wanted to look well, sad that it could not last. Although I feared that she would topple over at any moment, she never stumbled once. She managed to walk up two flights of stairs without a problem, and down stairs as well.

One of Jane's prettiest evening gowns gave me a fitting problem. She was a bit more plump than before she became ill. In my concern, I kept putting more food into her than she actually needed. So the orange and gray dress was too tight around the waist. What could I do? I had thread and sewing paraphernalia. But adjust a dress? My solution seemed to work: I left a couple of snaps unsnapped and covered them with her sash. Usually, I hate sashes—but thankfully this dress had one. Nobody, not even Jane, knew the difference.

We explored all the lounges on board. Our favorite was the Sky Lounge, high above the captain's bridge, where, sitting in the front of the ship, we could see 180 degrees from horizon to horizon.

Most passengers were polite to us as we passed them in the halls or lounges. But most of them did not care to visit with us or try to talk with Jane. I expected that, and understood. And I didn't blame them. They were all here to enjoy a cruise, so why should they spend unhappy moments?

Some, however, made a point of chatting with us, visiting whenever it seemed appropriate. To them, Jane beamed her sunny smile and welcoming eyes. She would nod her head and appear to understand what they were saying, and utter "hello" and "good-bye" at the right times. Often she would startle me with a reply that required genuine cognition. At such times my heart would leap and I'd wonder if by some miracle she could be getting better.

Every day, without fail, I made sure we walked at least a half-hour on deck. The seas were amazingly calm every day of the cruise. Yet a wind always seemed to blow, especially on the top deck. For a while, we would walk along the promenade deck. But we always seemed to be in the way of vigorous, purposeful couples who pumped away in their hurried walks and seemed, I thought, impatiently trying to pass us.

So I decided "the hell with them," and from then on we walked the top deck, challenging the wind each day. To keep Jane's hair from blowing (keeping her hair looking as attractive as possible had become a preoccupation with me), I put a rainbonnet on her head. Jane managed her walking very well, except for descending the outside stairway from the top deck. She simply was afraid to step down, even though she could hold on to the railing with one hand and I was holding her other arm. But we managed.

Our routine soon became quite fixed: After breakfast, we went up to the top deck for a half-hour of hitting golf balls in the cage, while Jane sat on a deck chair just out of the sun, watching me with a half-amused smile on her face, or dozing. After golf, we took our walk. Then to the Sky Lounge, where I would write for an hour or so and Jane serenely watched the ocean.

Then came lunch, followed by her nap. While she was

sleeping, I'd go down to the exercise room and ride the bicycle and pull the pulleys. Two strong, good-looking Swedish girls ran the sauna-massage section. Never having had a sauna, or a massage, for that matter, I watched in some curiosity as these girls rolled and kneaded the fat, mostly bald-headed men who seemed to think they were exercising. Since I was losing my hair, too, I didn't dwell too long on balding, but they were all fatter than I. On the other hand, some of the young men seemed to go at the exercises too hard. They would race the bicycles at top speed for perhaps ten minutes, then lift weights until they almost screamed in agony . . . then row hard for another ten minutes. I couldn't remember whether I did that sort of dumb thing at their age. I probably did. I was content, however, to use my Schwinn pulse-meter, to almost double my heartbeats, and to keep my heart beating at that rate for three sessions of eight minutes each. I interspersed the bicycle riding with exercising with the pulleys.

After her nap and my exercise, Jane and I would see a new movie, if there was a good one—or an old one we enjoyed seeing again. One of the oldies was *The Glenn Miller Story,* introduced by June Allyson, a passenger on board. Then we went to tea in our favorite lounge.

If we didn't see a movie we attended a lecture, or a musical recital. Often we sat in the library just reading. That is, I would sit and Jane would leaf through books. There were always more activities than we could possibly have attended. At each lecture or movie, and in the library, Jane was patient and seemed to pay attention.

Taking Jane to tea was especially enjoyable. She seemed to anticipate it and acted as if she were in her element. The ship's crew served the tea in beautiful china. For each cup I gave Jane two lumps of sugar instead of the Sweet 'n Low on board. Funny that the Royal Viking Line, so luxurious and sophisticated in most ways, seemed never to have heard of Nutrasweet's Equal.

With a flourish, a steward would roll up the cookie-and-cakes wagon. Seriously, yet with a half-smile, Jane would study the assortment carefully, mentally enjoying each one. Then came the decisions. I wanted Jane to enjoy her goodies, but not to spoil her appetite for dinner. Two cookies and one cake, or three cookies and one pastry, was the limit. That always seemed to suit her, and she would sit happily munching, sipping her tea, while gazing out at the gently rolling ocean.

Afterward we returned to the cabin to rest, or to see a program on our TV monitor. We then bathed for dinner. Getting ready for dinner was always a lengthy procedure. While Jane could wear slacks at breakfast and lunch, dinner was always a dress-up occasions, even on informal evenings. So it became a matter of diaper, rubber pants, then panty hose to cover everything, followed by a dress or blouse and skirt—and heels.

Since Jane became ill I haven't bought her any dresses. Those she had in her wardrobe are classics, well-made and well-styled, and serve admirably for all occasions. I probably brought along too many dresses (I don't know how to pack light) but Jane wore every dress.

Just before dinner, we joined the dancing and cocktail hour in the Main Lounge. Several couples knew they were excellent dancers and constantly displayed their prowess. At such times I regretted that Jane could no longer dance, for we'd have shown them what a real dancing couple could do. Such silly thoughts—but I still wish we could have danced the way we once did.

For Jane I'd order a 7-Up, and wine for me. Our favorite lounge waitress was MaryAnn, from Copenhagen. Like so many of the staff, MaryAnn took a special liking for Jane and we got to know her well. She spoke fluent English. We discovered that she wanted to become a writer and had even written something that had sold. Her special interest was writing poetry and passionate romances.

She asked for help and I did the only thing I could do: I encouraged her to keep at it, always. I urged her not to worry about complex language and big words, but to keep everything simple. Just say what she felt and knew.

At times I would take Jane in my arms and try to dance with her. I'd take her out on the floor and start a simple one-step march in time to the music while holding her in my arms. Jane would smile and seem to enjoy it as long as she gave herself to the music. The moment she started thinking about the dancing, and me, however, she'd lose the rhythm and stop.

As I knew she would, Jane went on every shore excursion. Such excursions were made easy for elderly people who couldn't, or wouldn't, walk very far. There would be a morning excursion by bus or automobile, then lunch, then an afternoon excursion. We managed at least one, and often two, excursions each day we were in port.

Most of our days, we treated the ship as a floating resort hotel. Although Jane and I enjoyed the shore excursions, we—at least I, and I'm sure Jane, too—often felt that the excursions were an intrusion on the enjoyable shipboard routines.

Sometimes, the local harbor forced us to anchor off-shore, so we had to depend on the ship's tenders to take us ashore. Jane would walk down the gangplank stairways to the platform for boarding, then shy away from the bobbing tender. Yet somehow she knew she had to step across the gap. I'd be holding her by the arm, and a ship's officer would take her other arm. Together, as we called out, "Here we go, Jane," she would step up and over as if she did it every day.

On bus trips we usually got on board first to sit in the back. Climbing up the bus steps was no big problem. But coming down was something else. Stepping down the bus steps frightened Jane. Since we were the last to get off, I didn't mind how long it took to reassure her and finally help her down. She always made it. The other passengers and Jane and I had worked out an informal method that suited them and us. Nobody except us waited, and we were used to waiting.

Several passengers took a proprietary attitude toward Jane, almost as if protecting her from me. I was delighted that they cared. On our visit to Tahiti, for example, our group was to walk up a hill to view a carved statue.

As Jane and I started walking up the hill, a man with a florid face, whom we had seen from time to time in the dining room, came up to me, his face more flushed than usual.

"Listen here," he said to me sternly. "You can't take her up there. It's much too far and steep for her to walk!"

I smiled at him and said thanks. "Really," I said, "she can go it easily. And it'll be good for her. She needs to walk as much as possible."

Grumbling, he walked off shaking his head. Nor did he turn back to see how Jane made out. Nobody else had any suggestions for us the rest of the trip—and we always managed.

We enjoyed Tahiti and we loved New Zealand and Australia. One of the best photographs ever taken of Jane, I think, was snapped while we were attending a formal reception at the Sydney Opera House. She was laughing, her blonde hair contrasting with her black and gold evening gown. I ordered several dozen prints to send to our sons, others in the family, and friends.

We flew home from Hong Kong, Jane managing that well, too, even though we sat in a middle section and had to change diapers in the cramped toilet areas. Yet despite her difficulty in understanding, in walking, and in moving in any way, Jane was graceful, serene, and composed, and seemed happy throughout the trip.

An on-board videotape crew filmed the entire round-the-world cruise. They offered passengers a "personalized" version, suggesting anywhere from eight to ten minutes to be focused on any passenger who bought a cassette. I ordered two, one Beta and the other VHS. I had the crew tape us in our usual routine—at golf, walking, sitting in the lounges or the dining room, with MaryAnn, Mybrit, Manuel, and Marino, of course, and in our cabin.

I decided on an experiment for the segment in our cabin. Jane sat beside me, playing with Teddy, the teddy bear Elizabeth Riley had given her. She seemed to listen and understand because she laughed in all the right places. My experiment was to talk into the camera, as if to my sons, for perhaps three or four minutes to see how it went. For some time I've thought of getting a camcorder to take family and travel cassettes—as well as to talk into the camera about Jane's life story and my own, for our sons and grandchildren. I know I always wanted to know more about my father and mother, and their ancestors. This, I thought, would be something our sons and grandchildren could feel a part of.

13

Better for Jane Alive — Than Dead

Shocked! That's only part of how I felt at the idea of taking that sweet, childlike wife of mine, the mother of my sons, into a nursing home.

Perhaps everyone who considers a nursing home for a loved one feels a sense of loss and guilt that is almost impossible to bear.

But I had to reach some decision. I could see Jane deteriorating and began to worry whether I could take care of her if she got worse. And she would, I knew, get worse. Much worse. Then, too, I wondered if a nursing home would even take her if she got much worse.

A large part of my concern was my own heart and how it would stand up. I felt good, as if I'd never had a heart attack. But I still didn't really know what was happening to me.

The decision, and the process, were agonizing.

Friends, our physicians, all advised me to enter Jane into

a nursing home. Some wondered why I hadn't done it long ago.

"You," they insisted, "are better for Jane alive than dead."

When I thought about it rationally I had to agree. Just the expression on Jane's face when I was with her told me everything. To her, having me with her in whatever ways, whatever times, was important.

Yet I realized that the effort and concern involved in taking care of Jane—for example, just the act of slowly pulling her upright, carefully sitting her down, worrying about everything that she couldn't talk about or respond to—produced the subconscious stress that had probably precipitated my heart attack several years ago.

I studied the prospect of getting a crew of nurses into our home to care for her. Although we have a two-story townhouse, we could easily rearrange the den as a bedroom. The toilet right off the den would be convenient. For a time, she could walk upstairs for her shower, I was sure. And then my reasoning began to break down—and I knew, even if it could be done, it would only be for a short time.

If I could live longer and take care of Jane longer and keep her happy as long as possible by entering her into a nursing home, I decided, then that's what I probably should do. Finally on May 20, 1985, I entered Jane into a nursing home right in Princeton.

Dear Alan, Guy, Paul:

Today I entered Jane into the Princeton Nursing Home. The dear, sweet, plucky little girl took it in stride. And I am still crying.

The best way to tell you the major reason for entering Jane into the Home is, as I've told you before, I have ischemic heart disease. How severe I do not know.

Now, here are my reactions: As I may have told you, I have my cholesterol down to 150. My HDL to LDL ratio is 1.9—and anything below 2 is excellent. So, as Leonard

Stone says, cholesterol is not my problem. My hope is that I might reduce the narrowing of the arteries, as Pritikin apparently did by following his low-fat diet. My weight is 170 and I will get that down closer to 165. (By low fat I really mean low fat. I've cut out *all* fat except for whatever is used in the whole-wheat bread I eat and in the fish and chicken I eat. On the advice of the AMA, I take one table-spoon of polyunsaturated oil and one tablespoon of monounsaturated oil [olive oil] per day in an oil and vine-gar dressing for my salad. Otherwise, no fat).

I've noticed, as the article also indicates, that when I sit at my typewriter for several hours or sit at my desk writing checks to pay bills, a tension tends to build in my chest. The article says these may be silent ischemic attacks, with cumulative damage. On the other hand, a month or so ago when several readings of my blood pressure showed a sudden rise, I had Leonard give me another EKG—and I asked him if I'd had a silent heart attack and didn't know it. He said "No, you didn't."

So, in a nutshell, I'm assuming the best—that my heart really is in good condition, that my diet and steady exer-cise will strengthen it, and that I can reduce stress—mainly by trying out having Jane in the Home.

As you might suspect, I have always enjoyed taking care of her. Sometimes the meals and dishes, etc., got a bit try-ing. But I realize that just taking care of her, changing her, changing the bed, washing, and so on and on, probably carried a lot of subconscious stress.

You should know, too, that my secondary reason for entering Jane—and it may turn out to be the most important—is to manage to get her into a home while she is "acceptable." Eventually, as you know, all Alzheimer's patients must go into an institution, if they live. And I think it is important to have Jane admitted now.

On the other hand, as I sit here wondering how she's taking eating a strange meal, being undressed for bed by a strange person, going to sleep in a strange bed with another woman in the same room—large and pleasant though the room is—I can tell you that it won't take much to get me to bring her back home and the hell with the ischemic heart disease.

When I left Jane, she was sitting on a couch in the big day room with another woman—and the room was filled with old men and women sitting in wheelchairs, all watching a big screen TV show. Jane was sitting placidly, watching, her legs crossed comfortably. She smiled when I came and sat down beside her and held her hand. After a little while I kissed her good night and said I'd see her tomorrow.

I will, of course, see her every day. I plan to sit with her during meals and to take her on her daily walk. At the very least I will drive her home, have some juice and a cookie, take our walk on our usual route, and then return her to the Home.

When I look at it objectively, I think perhaps Jane will enjoy it in many ways. The nurses are all young and, while I was there anyway, loving to her and the other patients. The assistant head nurse is a motherly soul who got on with Jane instantaneously. I must say the place looks just as good and as sophisticated as the Princeton Hospital, which by all accounts is an excellent place.

I took a look at the activities schedule—and it is full, with sing-alongs, moving to music, bingo, bowling, discussions, crafts, and so on. Jane will enjoy watching those things she cannot participate in.

And of course I've decided to keep her in her two-days-a-week Day-Care program for Alzheimer's, because the staff and volunteers and other patients have become her friends and she actually looks forward to being with them.

Actually, Jane will probably take this whole move much, much better than I, which makes me glad and breaks my heart.

Tonight I'm going to watch the Joanne Woodward TV show on Alzheimer's disease. It is ironic that her mother is a victim. I think the story will probably come closer to Jane's experience than anything else we have seen. I know now that Jane went through a period at ETS when people looked at her strangely, wondered if she were stupid and incompetent (thank God I didn't know it at the time or I would have been brought up on murder charges), and I agonize that I didn't realize, didn't know, couldn't help her through it. I can only believe that she really didn't know what was happening and was gradually insulated from pain. She talked to me only once about a sharp and offensive treatment by the Executive Vice President, Bob Solomon—and, as she talked rationally about it, I simply thought (which was true) that Bob Solomon was only being his rude, gauche, unfeeling self.

I'll stop now. Enjoyed seeing Alan during his business week in Princeton. Wish I could see you all, talk to all of you. Love you all.

P.S.: I should have added something about the likely causes of my heart disease if cholesterol is not my problem. Leonard Stone said that it could have been one or a number of things . . . genes, hormones, stress, or a combination of all three. Still, records show that nobody who has ever had a cholesterol reading of 150 has ever had a heart attack—no matter what the genes, hormones, stress, or cholesterol. So, I only wish I had been more stringent with my diet decades ago. That's always the case, of course.

Choosing a home was a job of turmoil. Many times, during nightmares and angry days, I declared that I'd picked the wrong one. Still, in most respects important to Jane—and, I felt, important to me—I thought I picked the right one.

I selected the Princeton Nursing Home, just three minutes' drive from our home. This would enable me to come in and out at any time, as often as I was needed and wanted to come. Mainly, I wanted to be able to bring Jane home every afternoon—and take her for walks to ward off that inevitable day when she'd have to go into a wheelchair.

This nursing home was more expensive than some located farther away but was certainly not the most expensive in the state. A private room wasn't available. So Jane entered a room holding two other elderly women. Each patient had her own closet with a tiny chest of drawers. One toilet, one sink, one toiletries cabinet. Beside each bed was a nightstand with drawers. The room seemed barren, sterile, like a hospital room.

My mind raced with imagined terrors Jane might face. Being undressed and put to bed by strangers . . . taken to the toilet by aides who didn't know or understand that soft, slow motions got the quickest response from Jane. For months after she entered the home, Jane seemed afraid to go to the toilet. Then I found out that a nurse, whom I like and know to be conscientious and hard-working, had arm-locked Jane, during her early reluctance to sit down, and forced her on the toilet.

My rage at the nursing home administrators mounted as each day passed. In the first place, I was paying full rate for Jane—without help from either ETS or the government. Yet the place was filled with patients on Medicaid—paying rates substantially cheaper than what I was paying, as well as living off my taxes. Yet as a private payer, I got neither a single privilege nor extra care for Jane. In fact, it seemed to me Jane was being given the short end.

I take Jane to her hairdresser once a week for a shampoo and set. She loves the process and I sometimes think it's the best therapy she has. Women throughout the nursing home keep complimenting Jane on how beautiful her hair looks. Yet the aides seem not to know how to comb her hair. Often, in getting her up in the morning, they will deliberately wet her hair to comb it—or let it get wet while giving her a shower. Wetting her hairdo, of course, destroys her set and frizzes her hair out of control. Again and again I ask the administrator to instruct aides not to wet her hair, just comb it. But nothing seems to work— and I keep paying them for such service!

Day after day I'll arrive at the nursing home to take Jane home only to find her sitting, sopping wet, in a chair where she's undoubtedly been sitting wet for hours. Again, I rage at the administrator about the aides— unsupervised aides, sitting on their butts watching television in the dayroom when I'm paying them well to change my wife's diapers every two hours. Not too much to ask, it seems to me.

Our worst experience, however, was over Jane's eating. During the first three months at the home I simply assumed that Jane was being fed appropriately. The food was competent, not distinguished, but competent. Canned vegetables, instead of fresh, and full of salt. Very little fruit, mostly puddings for dessert. But plenty of skim milk.

At mealtimes, I left Jane to the services of the staff during those first few months. They were supposed to feed her as a routine part of their work. I didn't check on it—and those are three months I wish I could take back. I will always remember them.

Jane was repulsed by the way the aides shoved food at her—as they did to other patients. She would turn her head away if they pushed food at her too rapidly. True, Jane is a slow eater and likes to take time chewing her food. But the aides seemed to feel the need to feed a patient in five or six minutes, then sit on their idle backsides for an hour or so watching television.

Finally, like an unobservant dolt, I realized that Jane had been losing weight. I noticed it first as I was changing her diapers at home—her buttocks, usually firm and in good shape, were sagging into large folds of skin. Alarmed, I checked with the nurses—and they finally weighed Jane. Sure enough, she had lost fifteen pounds. The nurses seemed unconcerned.

I was shocked—and furious at myself for not knowing, for not making sure of her eating. Thankfully, I had been feeding Jane so well at home that she already weighed perhaps fifteen pounds more than she ever had. So the weight loss was more of a warning than anything else.

I decided I would feed Jane. So I began a routine I continue to this day—feeding Jane at every meal possible. Slowly, Jane began to learn to eat for some especially compassionate aides. She would eat a good breakfast of two scrambled eggs, toast, jelly, hot cereal, three prunes, and two glasses of milk. Even so, on Tuesdays and Thursdays, the days for her day-care center, I found it wise to arrive at 8 A.M. and feed Jane breakfast, if only to get her ready to go in time.

Feeding Jane at lunch and dinner took my concentration. Always slow in eating, often finicky, Jane was nevertheless in general a delight to feed. We developed special little habits, sometimes even games to get her to eat. At times, when Jane would seem to refuse a mouthful of dental-soft meat, I would take the spoon and pretend to dip it into a nearby dish of dessert, or into an empty glass—anything to vary the routine. At once, Jane's mouth would fly open and she'd take the bite.

As a supplement to her eating, nursing home physicians prescribed Ensure, a liquid food supplement with all electrolytes, for Jane four times a day. In checking with experts, I found that Ensure is regarded as a good product.

At each meal, at my insistence, Jane had a piece of whole-wheat bread. I'd break it into little pieces, dip each piece in milk, and feed it to Jane with my fingers. She liked this procedure immediately—and it became our regular way of being sure Jane got her cereal at each meal.

Slowly, I got Jane to eat good meals. Her weight came back and now she weighs the same as she did when she entered. We continue to give her Ensure, because we don't know when the real, inevitable eating problems will emerge. We want to keep her weight as normal as possible—as long as possible.

After she regained her weight, Jane looked good—so good, in fact, that friends remarked that she really looked better than she had in some years. Her face and complexion were clear. She looked as young as she did ten years ago.

In many ways, my big battle at the nursing home is against myself. Too often I'm abrasive in the face of sloth, inefficiency, and the simple failure to fulfill routine duties for which I'm paying handsomely. My battle is to keep myself from raging so out of control that I might alienate Jane from the staff. I'm not asking for extras. I rage at the stupid, unnecessary problems: the loss of an expensive comb . . . disappearing toilet articles . . . stolen clothes . . . carelessness in cleaning and bathing her . . . not washing her teeth . . . consistently getting water on her hair . . . haphazard dressing . . . hurried feeding . . . and worst of all, leaving Jane sitting for hours in puddles of urine.

On those days Jane attended her day-care center, I wanted her to be dressed as well as possible. Somehow, the aides always managed the most god-awful combinations: black slacks, for example, but white socks and tan shoes. I asked—again, and again, and again—if they would please dress her in black slacks, black socks, and black shoes, or tan slacks, tan socks, and tan shoes. But no, it was always some dreadful mixture.

Too often, as I picked up Jane's dirty clothes to wash at home (I mainly wanted to keep track of her clothes), I'd find that aides had tucked socks worn the day before into shoes, to be used again without washing. Or, although I'd put four pairs of shoes in Jane's closet, so she'd have a different pair each day, the aides would put the same pair of shoes on Jane for days in a row.

My battles at the nursing home came to a head when, after the first year, the home administrator announced that he was increasing the cost of Jane's care. I could afford it—but that wasn't the point. I felt Jane wasn't even getting services for which we were already paying a great deal.

"You don't even give her the routine care I've been paying for," I said, as scathingly as I could. "How can you rationalize charging more?"

He shrugged his shoulders and replied: "We live in an imperfect world."

Many times I considered taking Jane into another home. For some time I've been investigating Presbyterian Homes' Meadow Lakes, an elite retirement center about ten miles away from our home. It's attractive—but I'm ambivalent about it. I'd have to move there myself, and I wasn't—and am not—sure that I'm ready for a retirement home, pleasant though it may be. On the other hand, I also realize that too often people put off going into such a place for too long. Suddenly something happens, or they realize all at once that they have to move—and it must be done quickly. Few of us ever really plan well in such matters.

I made lists of good things about it, and things I didn't like. First of all, Jane and I would be close. Much of her time could be spent in our apartment. I liked that. We could eat many of our meals together. Much time and racing around could be saved.

On the other hand, I was put off by the prospect of eating their food. I'm cooking my own meals free of saturated fats and salt and with a minimum of polyunsaturated fats. And in any institution, no matter how well handled or how individualized food preparation may be, how can you really be sure to get the food that is calculated to keep you alive?

So, each time I've decided to keep Jane in this nursing home—for now. We have managed, are managing. The home is finally buying the proper-sized Attends for Jane, and the aides are changing her so that most of the time she doesn't sit in pools of urine.

I like the nurses, all of whom are able, efficient, and concerned about the patients. They still spend so much time on paperwork, and handing out medications, they can't supervise the aides appropriately. But now they are all so aware of me and my insistence that Jane get what she's supposed to get that the routine is adequate.

Crippled though she is, Jane's personality and innate sweetness have won everybody over. Literally everybody, from the cleaning personnel and kitchen crew to nurses and administrator, all love Jane. Says one Latin aide: "She's our little angel."

In winter, I take Jane for walks inside the nursing home. She stoops more, takes shorter steps, talks less. We have a routine: We walk down the front hall to the main day room, circle through the room, stopping to exchange greetings with patients in wheelchairs, then head back down the hall to the kitchen. There we stand at the door, looking in. Jane seems fascinated by the huge stove, the machines, the bustling staff, the carts with trays for each patient. The cooking staff, especially the two burly cooks, one tall with a beard, the other short and jolly, wave to Jane and call out to her, "Hi, Jane. How are you?" She smiles, nods—and then we turn to continue our walk.

From the main floor we walk up two ramps to the second floor. Months ago Jane created a game in walking up—marching to an internal tune or sense of rhythm. On the second floor, we go into the accounting department and stop at the door, where Jane says hello to the staff.

The office manager, Rita Macken, thoughtfully and in fun has stashed a supply of fish-shaped cookies for Jane. At each visit, she gives Jane one little cookie. For some reason, either the jolly kidding of the office manager or her tone of voice, Jane responds more to her than to any other person and, in turn, tries to joke with her. Jane laughs and utters some exclamations, usually unrelated to the conversation. But by manner and tone, she seems to think she knows what she's saying. At such times, I feel that inside her brain Jane knows precisely what joke or funny comment she's uttering. It's just that it doesn't come out right. I know she's joking because it's precisely the way she used to joke when well, leading me to believe that there is still a lot of cerebral activity in her brain.

From the accounting department we walk into the therapy room—a room Jane has made her fun room. First, we stand in front of the full-length mirror. Jane makes little faces at herself, talks to herself in a delightful remonstrating manner. Then we walk around the room, Jane oohing and aahing at the machines, at the pictures of little boys on the wall.

At the end of the therapy room, where we can see ourselves in the full-length mirror, we start walking toward the mirror. Jane started another game some time ago. As she starts to walk, she breaks into a march—marching toward the mirror to some internal tune in her mind. As we wind up before the mirror, she salutes.

Her salutes delight me—and break my heart. With a smile, and a flourish, Jane salutes—but her hand never reaches her eyebrow. It stops somewhere near her chin or ear. But it's a salute. In her eyes, it's the joy and triumph of doing something that's fun.

From the therapy room we go on down another hall past the chief engineer's office—which, for some reason, seems especially fascinating to Jane. Then we go through the laundry room, where the huge washers and driers are always rumbling. We check out the storeroom, where new underpads, towels, sheets, disposable towels, and cloths are stored—a room that smells clean, probably from the powder used in packing.

At times, when the intercom is playing dance music, a familiar tune will come out of the speaker overhead at the end of this hall. At those times, Jane breaks into a marching dance step, her face rapt in the rhythm. I step along with her, hand in hand. Sometimes I take her into my arms to dance as we used to dance together so often. Again, I weep inwardly at the memories of dancing with her. She clings to me as she always did, and we simply lose ourselves in a slow, one-step dance to the rhythm and music.

Then we walk back down the hall to the ramp. In going down, Jane started another little game of counting her steps. Clearly and forcefully, Jane would count—up to sixteen.

Once, a few months ago, my heart leaped again when we started down this ramp. After a few counts, Jane realized that she was mixed up.

"Wait a minute," she said, instantaneously. Then she started counting over again from the beginning. That, I was convinced, took some cognitive doing—to realize she was making a mistake in counting, say "wait a minute," and then start over.

Sad to say, she has not done that since . . . and her counting becomes less clear. A year ago she couldn't make it beyond nine. And today—well, more about that later.

Going down the second ramp is different. We march down that ramp to my rhythmic words of "Dar-ling, dar-ling, mar-ching Jane. . . ."

And then we repeat the walking route as often as we can before Jane gets too tired. I'm convinced that aides would rarely, if ever, walk her. The only regular, appropriate walking she gets is with me.

A year ago, we could make five or six trips around that circuit before Jane would get tired, never seeming to get bored. But the circuits gradually diminished.

When the days are warm and sunny, I take Jane for a walk outside. We slowly make our way from the nursing home to Witherspoon Street and a half-block to a drugstore. We slowly walk through the aisles, looking at the bright red, white, blue, and green boxes.

Should Jane be in the nursing home at all?

This is a question I put to myself again and again, almost every day. We're taught to keep family members at home, where they are loved and cared for so well, just as long as possible. And indeed, were it not for my heart attack, and my concern about my situation, I would be caring for Jane at home—with daily help, of course—just as I did for years before and after her diagnosis.

All I can say is that even though I felt that I cared for Jane very well, and she was happy here, I think she looks better since she's been in the nursing home. Her weight is better. Her skin looks better. She seems livelier and talks better, more often, and even seems to think better in the nursing home than she did at home.

One reason she seems more responsive in the nursing home, I believe, is that the nurses and aides always speak to her with a smile—and challenge her to respond. They ask her questions in loud voices, as if requiring an answer, and Jane responds.

"Hello, Jane," a nurse will call out. "How are you?"

Jane will pause a moment, as if thinking, then smile and answer, "Hello. I'm fine."

So we walk—and walk. Sometimes we go out to ETS and walk around those spacious grounds. From the look on her face, I think Jane knows where she is and remembers the time she worked there. I tell Jane that we walk "to exercise her musk-kles" and she seems to go along with it, possibly understanding that the exercise is good for her.

At times, in the nursing home, I'll pretend to forget our usual route and start to walk past the kitchen or the accounting department just to see if Jane will remember. She always does. She will tug at my hand, or utter the word "here" and point to make sure we go in, for example, to get her fish cookie.

In the years of her illness before she entered the nursing home, Jane would walk with me along Nassau Street. Rarely, if ever, would she look in the store windows we passed. Yet a year or so after going into the nursing home, she began to stop to inspect the newest women's clothing displayed in the shops. From time to time she will tug my arm to take her into a shop. Once inside, she seems tentative, confused, not knowing what she wants or what to do. I stand with her a few moments, then she willingly turns and goes out with me.

On Nassau Street, Jane remembers the time we went into Burger King for coffee. At each walk afterward, she would tug my hand in the direction of the Burger King door.

She likes to stop in the Greenhouse Room of the Nassau Inn for toasted bran muffins and coffee. By now the waitresses know us and welcome us with special smiles.

On winter evenings, after dark, I drive Jane back to the nursing home from visits to our house. The amber lights of the Nassau Inn, the parking garage, and the nursing home will shine in the darkness. Jane will often exclaim, "Isn't it pretty?"

How deeply pleased I am when Jane speaks phrases like "Isn't it pretty?" Phrases that I can understand. I look and hope for every evidence that Jane's mind is working. So I cherish every bit of talking, every time she expresses enjoyment or says that she loves someone or something. All show that life still has some meaning for her.

Yet I despair. The sorrow is always unbearable—always! I realize that I still have not come to terms with the enormity of this tragedy. I enjoy being with Jane, yet I know there must always be decline. A year ago she could walk two miles; today she becomes exhausted after three blocks, and her steps become ever slower and shorter. Yet she steps over cracks in the sidewalks, up curbs and steps, whatever is required, with surefooted strength and confidence.

When we're together I'll hug her and give her a series of kisses and repeat what we have said to each other so many times: "We'll just do the bestest we can."

14

The Last Vassar Reunion

Taking Jane to her forty-fifth Vassar class reunion was important to both of us. The final occurrence of anything in life seems to be an exclamation point. I wanted it to be an event, a memorable event. Jane, of course, had no sense that it was anything but just another meeting with friends. Perhaps I sentimentalized things too much.

Taking her to the reunion was a real logistics challenge.

First, it took planning and some resolve. It would be so easy to say, "Why bother? She wouldn't understand—or enjoy anyway." Yet somehow I couldn't. I didn't feel driven, or guilty, or have any similar feeling. I just wanted to take her to the reunion and felt it was important—and that she'd enjoy it. It was 1985. She was walking in slower, mincing steps, but seemed to recognize good friends and say a few phrases.

As usual, we had a special hair appointment the day before. Jane always knows when her hair is looking good and I wanted her to feel that her hair was well done. Getting the big car ready for the drive up to Poughkeepsie was one of those nuisance types of "must." I wanted no breakdown with Jane in the car.

Because we wanted to make an early start, I brought her home from the nursing home and at about 8 P.M. I washed her teeth, took her to the toilet, arranged underpads on the bed and clean diapers on her, then tucked her in. I told her where we were going, but I'm not at all sure she understood. Still, she trustfully sighed and smiled.

Jane awoke early the next morning, as she always did before a trip. Her eyes, shining with excitement as if sharing a secret with me, peered at me over her covers as she waited for me to wake up. "I love you," were her first words that morning, and she smiled. I leaned over and gave her a bunch of kisses.

After toileting her, I gave Jane a shower and laid out her clothes. Since it was raining, I said the hell with the dress and dressed her in black slacks, a white blouse, and a black sweater. With her golden hair a contrast to the black, she looked young and attractive. I was confident she'd look all right for the reunion, not knowing, of course, how all the other women would dress.

We took off in the rain, certain to arrive in time for Saturday's main events. But as I drove out of Princeton, I realized I'd forgotten Jane's bag of toilet articles, diapers, clean rubber pants, fresh slacks, and socks.

Cursing myself for my forgetfulness, I turned back to the house—wondering, as I often do at such times, if I'm coming down with Alzheimer's myself. Well, so what if we were late? We'd still see a number of Jane's friends.

Later, I cursed myself again for forgetting an umbrella. By the time we reached Poughkeepsie, the rain was insistent, bent on continuing.

Jane, I determined, would not arrive at her reunion drenched. So for over an hour I drove through the business districts of Poughkeepsie looking for an open store selling umbrellas. I found one in a shopping center that had no parking. Several blocks away, I found a place to park and asked Jane earnestly to stay right there and not move. I'd be back soon, I told her. Not knowing what the area was like, I locked the car doors, knowing full well that under some circumstances it would keep out people who'd try to help Jane instead of hurt her. My odds were better this way, I decided, and hurried off in the rain. I got the umbrella all right—a big, red-and-white golf umbrella, more expensive at $75 than I wanted to spend, but it would certainly keep the rain off. As with so many elitist expensive things of that kind, everything worked well—except the spring for the little lever that held the umbrella open. So it kept slipping, letting the umbrella collapse. There it was—just another piece of junk.

We arrived at the Vassar campus, finally. At the gate I got advice on where to park for the field house. I'd changed Jane at a gas station on the way up to Poughkeepsie, so I knew we were good for several hours before I needed to change her again.

We parked and headed for the field house, along with a throng of women and men headed through the rain in the same direction.

As we entered the field house, I could see at once that alumnae were gathering in separate sections of the arena, under large signs reading, for example, "Class of '41." When we approached, Jane's face already bore a smile of anticipation. A dozen of Jane's classmates recognized her. Shouting and calling her name, they descended on her. There was a long round of hugging and kissing and crying. I stood off at the side, watching . . . so glad that they welcomed Jane enthusiastically, yet crying inside that it had to be this way.

Several classmates whom I've known through the years came over to say hello to me. Each of them remarked, "Jane looks so good!" For a few moments, I thought Jane had forgotten me. But every once in a while she would look over at me and smile.

Expressions on her face kept changing. In her gentle yet feisty manner, I could see that she was trying to make jokes with her classmates. They all seemed to understand and laugh along with Jane. But it was her manner, the sound of her voice, they reacted to, for her words were an incoherent jumble.

When the band began to play a march, a classmate took Jane by each arm. Together they marched at the head of their class. I watched Jane's face. She seemed transported. Sheer excitement and delight . . . and happiness . . . reflected in the way she laughed and bobbed her head in time to the march.

That was the high point of the reunion—an emotional, melodic, marching expression of joy with women she had studied with forty-five years before. Eventually, the marching music stopped. Classes moved into their seats for the "business" meeting. As usual, some honors were given, as well as some reminders about contributions to the college.

Next came box lunches. A number of classmates Jane saw most often at college brought their lunches over to sit around us. The conversation was gentle, kind, full of family news, what was happening to other classmates, how children were doing in college or marriage. There was sadness over classmates who had died.

The food was strange to Jane. She ate very little of the chicken nuggets, cole slaw, and apple. But she did enjoy the soda drink. By this time, I had stopped worrying about her eating. It wouldn't hurt her too much to miss a meal. I'd make up for it with some snacking on the way back, along with the juices and vitamins I'd brought along.

Saying good-bye was hard for everybody but Jane. I couldn't tell how much she had understood of the afternoon's activities. Perhaps she thought it was something that might happen again tomorrow. Her classmates hugged and kissed her. All said they'd be sure to see her at the next big reunion in five years—the big fiftieth. Yet there were shadows behind their eyes, regret and resignation that in another five years Jane probably would not be with them.

At times, Jane's thinking seems to improve. I ask myself: Can her brain really get better? I simply don't know. My feelings, my reading, tell me that it's impossible. The experts tell me that the degeneration of Jane's brain is a constant process. There are no real plateaus, no remissions.

Yet, as I've said, Jane has learned to count steps up to our bedroom.

Now, whenever we go up or down steps—wherever they might be—Jane with vigor and enthusiasm counts them. I sense her feeling of triumph whenever she finishes counting.

Often, as we drive the car through familiar routes, Jane will say, correctly, "Now turn left," or "Turn right here."

These instances of clear language and appropriate responses may be reflexive, of course. Perhaps portions of her brain unaffected by the Alzheimer's have taken over some of the simpler tasks. Perhaps, in our own fumbling way, we have trained other sections of her brain to pick up thinking and motor skills where the diseased part of her brain leaves off. If so, I'll always kick myself for not doing a better, more thorough job of it.

My heart always beats with pleasure whenever Jane talks or shows that she is thinking. The presence of other people, especially those who talk directly to her, nicely demanding responses from her, tend to encourage her to rise to the challenges.

When someone speaks forcefully to her, saying, "Hello, Jane. How are you?" Jane will answer, quick as a flash, "I'm fine." At the appropriate moments, Jane says hello and good-bye." When we're walking and meet someone who shows some little courtesy, Jane's immediate response is "Thank you."

One day recently, as I prepared to take her to her day-care center, Jane smiled at me, clasped my hand eagerly, surprised me by saying clearly, "Well, what are we going to do today?" But could it last?

When I return from a trip—and my trips are very short these days, usually less than a week to visit my mother or my sons—Jane, cared for while I'm away by community health service nurses, greets me with a welling up of pleasure and emotion. She will laugh and weep at the same time, clasping my face in her hands, kissing me, saying "Mommy, mommy, mommy" over and over again.

After such trips, as we sit holding each other's hands, she will look at me with her eyes soft and yearning and say, with emphasis, "I love you."

Much as I'd like to believe we're holding Jane's brain on a plateau, I know it just isn't so. Over the long run, I know she continues to decline. I can tell it from one three-month period to the next. Mentally, as I say, I'm prepared for it—but each time I recognize the change, I feel a shock. My heart just breaks, but we do the best we can.

When I'm with her, and we're walking in the sunshine, her hand eagerly clasping mine and a smile of anticipation on her lips, all's right with the world and I feel content.

That year, being away from the boys seemed especially poignant. I put some of my feelings in this letter:

Dear Alan, Guy, and Paul:
Still another Christmas comes. Even though we can't be with you in person, Jane's heart and love are with you and with your families. And my thoughts and heart and love are with you and all whom you love. I'm so pleased

that if we can't be together you are celebrating your own Christmas traditions with family.

As I've told you in our telephone conversations, I plan to take Jane to Amy's wedding in Cleveland. Amy is Nancy's youngest child. Jane will be able to see Nancy and Bob Brill again, Alice will be there, as will Bob, Jane's younger brother. I plan to drive, for Cleveland is only five-hundred miles (just across the state of Pennsylvania) and handling the airplane these days is just too difficult. The car travel is completely controllable and comfortable. I think we'll start out Saturday morning and probably arrive late afternoon or early evening in Cleveland. There is a pre-wedding dinner of some kind that Nancy wants Jane to attend, so we'll plan on that. We'll stay over Saturday night as well as Sunday night, then drive home on Monday. We will go in to Elizabeth Riley's for Christmas Eve dinner. Harold will be there. And we'll again show the movies we've taken of this group for the last forty-five years—along with the latest movies taken last year, when Jane got her gift of Teddy. Instead of staying overnight at Elizabeth's, we'll drive home right after dinner.

I haven't written you about Jane for what seems a long time. I can't really remember. Alan and Guy have seen her and spent time walking with her within the last few months, so you know pretty much how she is. Paul is planning to fly back for a visit sometime soon, although the operation he now faces for removal of the growth on his thyroid gland may set that back a bit. Perhaps he can come before he has the operation. In any case, he'll want to have the operation and make his visit probably during the slack times over the holidays.

In any case, Jane seems to be talking and thinking and responding to people somewhat better than she did several years ago prior to going into the nursing home. As I've said, I think perhaps it's coping with the nurses and patients, perhaps a feeling she's back in an institutionalized work place. We'll never know, will we? There are many hard things to bear, of course; I sometimes think the hardest are to realize, in feelings that seem increasingly to wash over me, that there is no return . . . there is no recapturing the past . . . that our lives are inevitably changed and there can only be decline. I've always thought I could handle change, since I understand it intellectually. But I find that emotionally Jane is so much a part of me that I simply can't bear the thought that there will be a time when she isn't there. All this, along with the remorse I feel over the many things I could have done, and should have done, to make her life easier and happier, are too often overwhelming.

I realize that such thoughts are no help in any way. So I spend most of my time, as you might suppose, feeding Jane, taking her for walks inside the nursing home when the weather is bad, taking her shopping with me at the grocery store, for she seems to like to push the cart and, I believe, feels she's helping me. At least I tell her so, repeatedly, and I think she believes me. I'm at the typewriter on my projects, never spending enough time on them. I find that I tend to turn down invitations. There were four invitations for Thanksgiving, which I turned down simply because I wanted to spend that day with Jane. But I talk with friends, go into New York for meetings and luncheons, and feel that I am not becoming a recluse. I read three or four papers regularly, skim a dozen magazines, have several books going at the same time, follow sports on TV. I'm doing my exercises regularly and feel very good. As I think I've told you, Dr. Fulmer changed my beta blocker from Tenormin to Pindolol. The only difference, really, is that Pindolol lets my heart beat about the 51-per-minute rate instead of the much lower rate of Tenormin. Dr. Fulmer tells me that my EKG, during my comprehensive physical a month ago, shows that my heart is getting stronger.

I'm still working to get all controllable fat out of my diet, for what's uncontrollable seems to be enough for nutritional requirements. Nutritionists have made so many mistakes through the years, and I've gone right along with them in making the same mistakes. It's pretty generally established now, though, that *fat can kill you.* Sugar and starches and carbohydrates will not kill you. But fat will kill you. The saturated fats will cause heart disease. The polyunsaturated fats, oxidizing as they do, will cause cancer. I'm only thankful that I've been taking the vitamins and minerals during these last forty years or so, for I think they have helped me through this period.

There is everything more to say . . . how you felt about the Dolphins beating the Bears, the problems of the Knicks, whether tax reform will really be reform, and get through . . . what the economy will be in the year ahead . . . what our planning is and should involve. Do take care and know that I love you more than words can express. Do give my love to Marilynne, Linda, and Marcia and give big kisses to Karin, Claire, Lisa, Daniel, Jenny, and Kate. I missed all their birthdays this year but will get back on the beam in '86. Have wonderful holidays—and I'll be there with you in spirit and in my thoughts.

Love,
Dad

15

THA: Our Last Best Hope?

Hope surged through me—again—in November of 1986. The hope was so strong it seemed to burst inside me because it promised so much and made so much sense.

Newspapers all at once were filled with stories emanating from *The New England Journal of Medicine*. In the November issue of this courageous medical journal was a report by a California neuropsychiatrist by the name of William K. Summers. For three years, the report said, Dr. Summers had been using a known but unapproved drug, THA (oral tetrahydroaminoacridine) on seventeen patients who had moderate to severe Alzheimer's disease.

In the first phase of the study, the report indicated, "significant improvement occurred in subjects who received the drug. . . . Among the 14 subjects completing Phase II, THA treatment produced significantly better results than placebo . . . no serious side effects attributable to THA have been observed. These encouraging initial results suggest that THA may be at least temporarily useful in the

171

long-term palliative treatment of patients with Alzheimer's disease. . . ."

I learned from the report that "the degree of improvement has often been dramatic. One subject was able to resume most of her homemaking tasks. One was able to resume employment on a part-time basis. One retired subject was able to resume playing golf daily. In other cases, there were improvements in activities of daily living, such as self-feeding at the family table, where total care had previously been required. . . . In several cases, proposed admittance of the participants to skilled nursing facilities has been forestalled. . . ."

Questions immediately began tumbling all over themselves in my mind:

It's not too late for Jane, is it?

Can I get Jane into the program?

What can I do to get Jane in?

What do other experts think of the THA report?

What are the chances of it's being a hoax? That question I answered myself: The *New England Journal of Medicine* is a highly respected professional medical journal. It would not publish a hoax.

Are there other experiments with THA being carried out nearer home? In the back of my mind, of course, was my worry at the thought of taking Jane across the country to California.

As quickly as I could I began to investigate.

First of all, I wrote Dr. Summers directly, both at his office in Arcadia, California, and at the famous Huntington Memorial Hospital in Pasadena.

Inside of a week, I received a polite note from Dr. Summers thanking me for my thoroughness in writing him at both places. His office enclosed a brochure entitled "Alzheimer's Treatment Research Project" conducted by Solo Research Inc., William K. Summers, M.D., Medical Director.

Every word in the brochure fascinated me. My hopes for help for Jane continued to rise. The whole process actually seemed possible. It could be done.

I made copies of the brochure and sent them off to Dr. Leonard Stone and Dr. David Fulmer, asking for their opinions. I asked them to be candid. They knew I wanted to get Jane into a valid program.

Then I studied the brochure itself. It was clear and persuasive.

The purpose of Solo Research's Alzheimer's program, it said, was to explore the long-term use of oral 1, 2, 3, 4 THA to reverse—in part—symptoms of Alzheimer's disease. The numbers 1, 2, 3, 4 indicated the different stages of the THA treatment.

The goals: In the short term, to improve the status of the known Alzheimer's patient. In the long term, to obtain approval by the Food and Drug Administration for use of the THA drug regimen in diagnosed Alzheimer's disease.

As for funding, the brochure emphasized that Solo Research was a private fee-for-service research corporation. Its mission was to make practical clinical research available to the public on a cost-of-project basis, with such costs being assumed by the participants.

"Because the drug THA was synthesized too long ago to be patented as a unique new substance, the drug industry has not been interested in funding the research," the brochure pointed out. "Government grants for research continue to focus on collecting and studying autopsy materials from Alzheimer's patients. The remaining viable method to fund the research is the fee-for-service model, which is gaining increased professional and lay support."

All of this seemed reasonable to me. So I turned to the listing of costs to see if Jane and I could afford the treatment. The figures were clear:

"Total cost first year—$12,100.00

"Total cost second year—$4,800.00"

The costs were broken down into schedules: Due forty-five days prior to appointment, $3,500. Due on date of first appointment, $2,000. Due at initiation of Phase II—$1,600. Due at beginning of fourth week. $1,000.

This also seemed reasonable to me. The total came to just about one-third of the cost of a nursing home for a year. And in a nursing home, the "treatment" is only custodial care. We had the money. By God we were going to spend it on helping Jane live better and longer.

Next, I studied the history and use of the drug, THA, as reported in the brochure.

It was first synthesized in 1908—and then ignored.

In the late 1940s, two Australian pharmacologists used laboratory animals to explore THA for possible uses. They discovered that animals put to sleep with large doses of morphine could be awakened and energized with THA— and that THA reversed the sleep effect and coma induced by a wide variety of drugs. It had generalized brainarousing capabilities. Toxic effects of THA were found to be minimal.

By the late 1970s, THA had not been further explored in clinical use until William K. Summers theorized the drug would be helpful in treating a broad spectrum of deliriums and dementias. Dr. Summers first used THA to reverse comas caused by suicidal overdoses. Later, he decided that THA might be helpful in the treatment of Alzheimer's disease.

In 1978, Dr. Summers began the use of intravenous THA in a pilot study of twelve Alzheimer's patients—nine of whom showed improvement of symptoms. Four of the nine exhibited dramatic improvement. However, within twenty-four hours of the administration of the drug, all patients returned to their original confused states.

Between 1981 and 1984, a blood assay for THA was developed. THA was shown to be safe for long-term use in laboratory monkeys and mice.

Then, in 1984, Dr. Summers started the first major study of THA on human beings—with important, gratifying results. In the next six months, more patients cautiously were added to the study.

This made so much sense to me. For decades, especially during the years in which I wrote articles and edited major magazines, I had always been fascinated by the cutting edge of medicine. I studied and tried to apply the creative process. I learned what went into discovery. So many discoveries were made in the way Dr. Summers seemed to be making this one with THA. So many courageous medical people had the guts to persevere in their theories.

I was ready. Were Jane able to comprehend, I was sure, she would be ready, too.

There was a disclaimer, of sorts. Dr. Summers made no bones about the fact that THA was not proposed as a "cure." Rather, it was a treatment to provide for medical management of Alzheimer's disease and to reverse some of its symptoms. The process is similar to the medical management of diabetes with insulin. Just as insulin is a symptomatic treatment, not a cure, and must be given daily, so the Alzheimer's victim needs THA daily.

Along with most of what I'd been reading, this made sense to me, too.

What about Dr. Summers himself? I desperately wanted him to be capable . . . an honest, creative medical man. But what about him, really?

Well, the brochure listed his professional credentials. Now I've long known that so-called professional credentials can be faked. Sometimes it takes intensive investigation to disclose the real facts. It was clear, however, that the professional credentials listed in the brochure could easily be checked.

Dr. Summers received his education at Washington University Medical School in St. Louis, Missouri, which I already knew to be an excellent medical school. He interned at Barnes Hospital and did his residency in internal medicine at Jewish Hospital and Stanford University Medical Center. He was a resident in neuropsychiatry at Renard Hospital in Washington University Affiliate Hospitals, with post-graduate studies at the University of Pittsburgh and Harvard University.

I was also impressed by the fact that his current hospital affiliations included Huntington Memorial Hospital, Pasadena, Methodist Hospital of Southern California, and Las Encinas Hospital, Pasadena.

He was, I concluded, an okay guy!

Now—could I get Jane into his program? If so, how would I go about it?

The answers to these questions were simple. The brochure told me to fill out a form that asked for information about Jane. Then I would take it to Dr. Fulmer to see if he would agree to take part in the project. Then he would send Jane's medical records to Dr. Summers. An appointment would be set for a first meeting with Dr. Summers. And we would plan to be in Los Angeles for about twenty-one days. The rest of her treatment would be given by her own physician back in Princeton.

Everything I could think of I put into motion to get Jane into Dr. Summers's program.

When I checked back with Dr. Fulmer about his thoughts on the THA program, he was quietly enthusiastic.

"I've read the material, Wood," he said. "It looks as if it's worth doing. I see no reason why you shouldn't move ahead with it. I'll be glad to write—and send Jane's records."

About the same time I received a call from Dr. Leonard Stone:

"Woody," he said, "I've checked around about this THA. And the people I've talked to say that there's really something to it. But it's so expensive. Charging twelve thousand dollars is outrageous."

"Yes," I agreed. "But—it's the only way I can get that treatment for Jane. It's worth it to us."

"Listen," he went on. "I'm told that Mount Sinai is getting ready to run a test on THA. Why don't you call and see if you can get Jane into that program? That way you can stay at home. It'll be a lot more convenient."

That sounded reasonable. After all, it would be better in

every way if we could get Jane on THA and stay at home. Perhaps the Mount Sinai program wouldn't be quite so expensive.

When I called the number Leonard had given me and spoke to the doctor, I immediately felt a foreboding. The doctor was kind but vague about everything connected with the study.

"My understanding is that the study isn't really going to be at Mount Sinai," she said. "It's going to be carried out with the Veterans Administration in the Bronx. My connection is only to obtain some volunteer patients. We don't really know when the study will get started, possibly early next year, maybe longer.

"But tell me," she went on, "how long has Mrs. Wirsig been ill with Alzheimer's?"

"Almost ten years," I said.

"Hmm," the doctor murmured. "Can she talk? Can she answer questions?"

"No," I replied. I sensed what was coming.

"Well, I'm sorry. I doubt that Mrs. Wirsig could be eligible to be in the study," the doctor said. Her voice was cool and confident, now. "The patients have to be able to respond to tests. That way we can measure whether the drug has done any good."

We were lost, I knew—but still I persisted. "But can't you tell whether there's been change? Or improvement? Simply by seeing whether there's better talking? Better walking?"

"Sometimes," she said. "But it's not accurate. It's not measurable. We have to be as certain of the results as possible. If I were you, I'd try very hard to get Mrs. Wirsig into the program in California. It's already ongoing. Maybe they have different criteria. . . ." Her voice trailed off, leaving me hanging.

That conversation, so unsatisfactory and discouraging, turned me back to Dr. Summers's program in California. My concern was rising.

"My God," I thought. "What if Jane *is* too far along? What if she can't get into Summers's program?"

Irrational thoughts kept running through my mind. It was unfair, I thought. Why couldn't victims get this drug while a test was being run on control groups? They were going to die, anyway. Why couldn't families decide whether their loved ones could risk any unknown dangers?

Worries began to keep me from sleeping well at night. I began to feel that Jane and I were victims of a conspiracy to keep us from obtaining help.

Why not call Dr. Summers's office to see if we could speed up a decision? I'd barely finished the thought when I put through the call.

"I'm going to be in Los Angeles on other matters," I found myself telling the woman on the other end of the telephone. "Could I come to the office to discuss my wife, Jane?"

"Dr. Summers is very busy," she answered, polite but remote.

"That's all right," I said. "I'd simply like to talk with someone about entering my wife into the program as quickly as possible. Her papers should already be there. Or arrive at any moment."

There was a pause. "Mrs. Wirsig's records are here," she said. "Everything seems to be in order. You don't really need to—"

"Oh, but I'm going to be there anyway," I said hurriedly. "I'll be there Monday morning at nine-thirty."

And I was. I'm always fearful of leaving Jane at the nursing home without someone special to take her for regular walks, and to see that she eats well, that she's kept clean—to make her feel that someone cares. By this time I've learned who among the aides are kind and thoughtful. One of them willingly tends to Jane's laundry, for which I pay her. Another takes Jane for walks each day, for which I pay her. And still another will feed Jane at the evening meals, for which I pay. The aides who feed her at breakfast and the noon dinner meal are very good. Even so, I try not to be away more than a few days at a time.

Dr. Summers's offices impressed me. They were in a modern-looking parklike complex of medical buildings in Arcadia, a few miles from Pasadena. Although his reception room was rather small, it was tastefully furnished and had a warm atmosphere. A fish tank, with colored fish swimming gracefully to the delight of patients, stood beside a door that obviously led into Dr. Summers's inner office.

The reception room was filled with elderly people who gazed at me with vacant stares. Were their thoughts turned inward on themselves? Or soaring back in time? How different from Jane's eyes, which always seemed aware of what was going on. There was no seat for me, so I stood, waiting.

When the receptionist was free to talk to me through her window, I assured her, "I don't really expect to see Dr. Summers. But I want to enter my wife in this THA program as quickly as possible."

"All right," the youthful, cheerful blonde woman said to me. She took out my folder.

"If possible," I went on, "could we make an appointment sooner than your regular forty-five days?" I didn't say that I was becoming more worried about Jane. It seemed to me she was just about to stop walking. More and more often she just sat in her chair, unthinking, it seemed, staring into space. I wanted her in the THA program just as soon as possible. It was now December 14, 1986.

The receptionist was scanning her calendar.

"Dr. Summers has a full schedule right up through January into February," she said. "How about February fifteenth?"

She saw the look of disappointment on my face. She turned back to her calendar, flipped some pages, then faced me again.

"He has a cancellation for January twenty-seventh," she said. "That's the best I can do."

"All right," I said. "Let's make it definite. January twenty-seventh at ten A.M. You'll want me to make the down payment, I assume?"

"Yes," she said. "Just make out a check for three thousand, five hundred dollars." And I did.

"Thank you," I said finally. "We'll be here the morning of January twenty-seventh. Bright and early."

16

The Battle with the FDA

In my Christmas letter to friends that December of 1986, I wrote:

> You who know and love Jane will be pleased for her this holiday season. A few days ago, she was accepted into the THA research program conducted by Dr. William Summers. His article in the *New England Journal of Medicine* in November, you may have noted, sparked a number of news stories and TV items. Jane's neurologist, usually cautious about such matters, is quite encouraged by the results Dr. Summers is achieving with his patients.
>
> Briefly, just to give you an idea of Jane's chances, Dr. Summers reports that to date 17 participants having Alzheimer's disease have started on THA, with 16 showing improvement. Two left the study for family reasons; 14 have continued to exhibit improvement *regardless of the severity of the illness*. This last is encouraging, for as you may know Jane has now been ill for almost 10 years and has been increasingly disabled for the last six years. The

181

THA drug is given orally. It is not a cure. Nor does it slow the progress of the disease. It enhances the neurotransmitter Jane may have left in her brain. She has so many windows of lucidity now that I'm sure she will benefit from this program. In a way, this drug will work for Jane the way insulin works for the diabetic.

We start the program at Dr. Summers's clinic in Arcadia, California, on January 27. We'll be staying at a private home in the area for 21 days while she undergoes treatment testing, monitoring. Then home for the program to be continued by her personal physician. We are hopeful. . . .

Again, logistics became one of my prime concerns. How could I be sure I would have enough Attends incontinent diapers out there—and in time?

And I dreamed again. Perhaps Jane could recover enough to recognize her sons. Maybe she could putt a golf ball again. Or chat with her friends. Or sail with me on another cruise. Perhaps—perhaps I could be sure she understood me when I tell her "I love you."

My hope was like tonic. I forgot the winter cold in making plans. Our son Guy's mother-in-law, Joan Martins, invited us to stay in her big house while Jane went through THA therapy. It was an ideal arrangement, for I'd traveled the route from her Sunland home to Arcadia in December. We could make it to Dr. Summers's office in twenty minutes, along one of the least-traveled freeways in the Southland. So much better than coping in a motel.

The trouble began, like a small cloud on the horizon, a week before we were to fly off to Southern California. One afternoon I received a call from an assistant in Dr. Summers's office.

"Mr. Wirsig, something's come up," she began. My heart began to pound. "It may change your plans, but I hope not. We've just received a telephone call from the FDA in Washington. We can't take any more patients—

not until Dr. Summers gets a letter from the FDA. It's supposed to spell out several things the FDA requires. . . ."

"You mean, we shouldn't come?" I asked, despair beginning to grip me.

"Perhaps hold off a week," she said. "The FDA said the letter was on the way. It should all be cleared up inside a week. If you wish, we can keep your appointment."

"But what's the problem?" I asked. "I can't understand why, suddenly, the FDA is doing this."

"Neither can we," she said. "Our whole office is in a turmoil. Dr. Summers has given the FDA all the material they say they want. He's even written a twelve-page letter to the President. . . ."

At that, my concern turned to worry. Only somebody who didn't know how to get things done would write a twelve-page letter to President Reagan, expecting him to help. I felt a strong twinge of doubt.

"Suppose we hold to our schedule," I said to Dr. Summers's aide. "We have our reservations. Our plans are all made. We might as well come on out. That way we'd be ready when the FDA says okay."

"Fine," she said brightly. "We're sure it's okay. It can be cleared up right away. . . ."

I'd planned our arrival in Los Angeles about four days before the January 27 appointment with Summers. With my fingers crossed, I'd ordered Attends and underpads for Jane's bed ahead of time, to be delivered in Sunland. Would they be there when we arrived? I fervently hoped so.

Now Jane was at the point of walking with short, stutter steps. She couldn't walk for long before we had to stop, let her rest, and start out again. Soon, in a tense effort to walk the way she wanted to, Jane would break into quick stutter steps again, almost pitching forward on her face. Sadly, I arranged for a wheelchair at Newark Airport—and another wheelchair at Los Angeles International.

We would fly out on United Airlines, first class. That

way I could be sure to be able to take her to the toilet when necessary. I wanted to have a toilet available when she needed changing. So the round trip cost $3,000. It was worth it. This was going to be our main chance to help Jane hang on to some of her life. It was worth anything . . . everything. . . .

Until we got to Newark Airport, I hadn't realized we were flying just before the Super Bowl game in Pasadena. But I learned soon enough. The airport was bedlam. Giants caps on Giants rooters seemed to be everywhere. All were heading for planes to take them to the game in the Rose Bowl.

Jane, a half-smile on her face through all the noise and confusion, sat waiting placidly with me for boarding to begin. We began to talk with a young couple going to the game—she a pretty blonde swathed in fox furs from neck to ankle, he a big, handsome young man who looked as if he had been a football player himself. As it turned out, he'd been a quarterback on the Princeton football team only a few years before. Now he worked on Wall Street. They sensed immediately that Jane and I had a problem. Could they help us on board, they asked?

Once again, as I had so many thousands of times, I was proud of the way Jane rose to the occasion. She couldn't talk, couldn't understand, was fearful of the noise, couldn't walk well . . . yet she seemed to understand when I asked her to help me stand her up. With visible effort she helped me get her up from the wheelchair. Then, in tortured steps, she walked down the first-class aisle to our seats. Our new friends offered to carry our flight bags. Thanks, I assured them, but I had to be able to do this all alone. I felt that I could—but, if necessary, I'd be sure to call on them. As it turned out, they sat behind us—and we talked often on that nonstop flight to Los Angeles.

As I suspected, the couple had been married so recently they were still caught up in the wonder of love and commitment. They kept referring to how much they admired the way I was caring for Jane. Obviously, they said in wonder, I loved her very much. While I was pleased that they thought so, talk of that kind embarrasses me. Down deep inside me I have the unspoken feeling that there is more to do—there must be more that I can do. We all agreed that after we returned home we'd have dinner some evening at the University Club.

Guy met us at the airport with a wheelchair and we made our way to Sunland without a snag. Guy and his mother-in-law had prepared Jane's bed, so all we had to do was take her to the toilet, change her diaper, oil her hips, thighs, and groin, and pop her into bed.

Wide awake now, Jane's eyes as usual peered at me from the covers, a smile on her face. She said, "I love you."

Watching the Giants thrash Denver in the Super Bowl was gratifying. But underlying the whole day was a sense of dread about what tomorrow and Tuesday would bring. Sure enough, my uneasiness increased when I called early Monday morning to confirm our Tuesday appointment. The aide I'd been dealing with was not there. Another woman explained that they had still not received the letter promised from the FDA weeks ago. So everything was still on hold.

"Did you want to see Dr. Summers anyway?" she asked.

"Well, yes," I said. "That's why we're here. Surely there must be something he can do while we're waiting for that FDA letter."

"All right," she said. "Come in at nine A.M. One of Dr. Summers's associates will talk with you and Mrs. Wirsig."

"Yes," I said. "But we're here to talk with Dr. Summers."

"Oh, yes," she said. "You'll see him afterward."

Caring for Jane again seemed to involve infinite details. On Sunday, I'd shopped for baby food, making sure I had a combination of cereal, protein, complex carbohydrates, fruit. It was going to be tough, I knew—three meals a day, changing, washing, walking. Would the stress get to me? I didn't know—and subconsciously, I guess, I didn't care. Besides, if I just took things slowly, took plenty of time even in putting on a shoe, I could do it all without too much of a problem.

Tuesday morning—D day for our new hope for Jane—I got Jane up at 6 A.M. It sounds simple, even to me. But washing her, combing her hair, dressing her, fixing breakfast, and getting her ready to travel took a good two and a half hours. Again there was absolutely no trouble. As always, Jane accommodated me at every step of the way. In her way, she tried to help and be cooperative. It just took time. Sometimes just getting a sock on seemed to take an interminable amount of time.

We arrived for our appointment at nine, on time. The office was not open. We waited in the car for perhaps a half hour, then tried the office again. It was open. We entered and sat down. A woman behind the receptionist's window said hello. We sat and sat and sat, while patients came in the door, went into the inner office, and came out again and left.

We had been waiting an hour when a youthful woman came striding in with an air of authority. She entered an inner office and soon began to run the copying machine. By eleven o'clock, after I'd inquired several times about our appointment, we were ushered into this same young woman's presence. She, it turned out, was a psychologist. She would give us a "preliminary" interview prior to our seeing Dr. Summers.

In a halting, confused, and obviously unprepared manner, she began asking us the most obvious, most mundane questions. None really focused on Jane's specific situation. With a sinking feeling in my stomach, I felt she was stalling for Dr. Summers. Was she just taking up our time while he finished with other patients? Perhaps he and his office staff weren't even expecting us.

Was this to be the procedure? If so, Jane and I weren't getting our $3,500 worth.

When the young woman realized that, ignorant as I may be about so many things involving Alzheimer's, I still knew as much as she did, or even more, we soon ended the interview. With a smile she said that I'd been very helpful. Then she said, "I'm sure that THA will be of great help to Jane." At that, I was ready to forgive her everything. She assured me that Dr. Summers would see us soon.

At last, almost three hours late, we met Dr. Summers at his office door. He ushered us into his office. It was a large room, luxuriously furnished, with a row of computer terminals lined up behind him. Impressive certificates covered one wall, sharing space with a nautical clock. Jane sat in one leather chair facing Dr. Summers across his desk. I sat in another beside her.

We waited.

"I'm not going to give THA to Mrs. Wirsig," he said right off.

His remark hit me hard. Failure once again, I thought.

"The FDA seems to be killing my whole project," he went on. "I can keep on giving my present patients THA—at my own expense. But I can't add Mrs. Wirsig to the group. Or any other new patients."

"But—but we entered Jane in the middle of last December," I said. "She was already accepted by you more than a month before this FDA action."

"Sorry. It doesn't seem to matter," Dr. Summers said. "They ask for toxicity reports. I've already sent them in. Somewhere at the FDA, under somebody's papers on a cluttered desk, lie my toxicity reports. . . ."

Anger often makes me see things, and especially say things, I later regret. I recalled the *Wall Street Journal* editorials criticizing the FDA's bureaucratic intransigence about drugs that could be saving lives. Here Jane and I were, caught in the same kind of maze, unable to move—with

help just a few steps away. I was ready to blow up at somebody, something—but I made myself speak slowly and
stay calm.

"Is there any way I could get hold of the drug directly?"
I asked. "And then give it to Jane under your direction?"

"No," he said, startled at my suggestion.

It was then that I noticed what he looked like, his man-
ners, the way he spoke. He was large, almost burly man
with hair somewhat tousled. With his glasses, the hair
made him appear almost like a grown-up Tom Sawyer, or
the way I imagined Tom Sawyer to look. He had a bold,
sweeping way of talking and acting, almost macho, somewhat defensive. I quickly learned that he was given to
quick, sweeping judgments made in a cautious manner.

"Well, what can we do?" I asked.

"Nothing," he said flatly.

I waited. This can't—it simply can't—be the end, I
thought.

"What we *can* do," he said, "is put Jane through some
tests. We could begin treating her with Pilocarpine. It's not
nearly as good as THA. But it has helped some people."

"Is there any way to move the FDA to act? Or change its
mind?" I asked. "Can we get them to move faster?"

"I don't know," he said. "They've got an investigator sitting in my office spying on me right now. He comes in
every day to inspect our records. To see what we're doing.
And then, I suppose, report back to Washington."

"There's something strange about all this," I said. "If the
drug is unsafe for Jane to take, why is the FDA letting you
go ahead with all your other patients?"

"The FDA okayed my research with these patients," he
said. "As far as I can see, after several years, THA is safe.
Now the FDA will goddamned not stop me. They're my
patients. What I say goes. The FDA will play hell stopping
me."

I watched the anger in his face and felt even more at a
loss.

"When do you expect the letter?" I asked. "And then, what do you think the letter will ask you to do?"

He laughed bitterly. "It was promised two weeks ago. But it isn't here. I called Washington yesterday. The letter hasn't even been put in the mail. When do I expect it? I can't tell you. What will it say? They want animal studies—and I'm not going to waste my time on animal studies when I have three years of toxicity reports on human beings."

I sighed and reached a decision. "If you will, I'd like you to put Jane through all the tests you planned. And begin to treat her with the Pilocarpine. Then maybe the FDA will relent."

We began a daily appointment program. I began giving Jane the Pilocarpine in prune juice, continuing to take her for walks, and put her to bed for naps in the afternoon.

Dr. Summers gave her a thorough physical examination. Then he scheduled a series of blood tests at the Huntington Memorial Hospital.

Next came a magnetic resonance imaging of her head.

I will always remember our meeting in his office following those tests.

"Jane," he began, "also has Parkinson's disease. That's why she's been walking with such difficulty. And her shaking hands. Have you noticed?"

"Yes," I said, my heart sinking. Parkinson's. "But it hadn't even occurred to me that she also had Parkinson's."

"And the magnetic resonance imaging shows a section of her brain just riddled with tiny strokes," he went on. "It may be that her talking problems stem from the strokes more than from Alzheimer's."

"But she does have Alzheimer's?" I asked. I don't know why, but at that moment I felt that something might be done for Alzheimer's, but strokes baffled me. I wanted Jane to have something that something could be done about.

"Yes, yes, of course," he said. "But you know—we can't

be absolutely sure about Alzheimer's until autopsy. At least now."

He paused for a moment, reading further in the memo before him.

"She also has had infarction in her brain stem. And one of the blood tests confirms what I had suspected. She also is suffering a mood disorder."

I cried inside. My poor little Jane's troubles were mounting. How could we ever cope with such problems? By now the Alzheimer's and possible assistance with THA were of almost secondary concern.

"We'll give her Sinemet for the Parkinson's," he said. "Sinemet contains L-dopa, one of the brain's neurotransmitters. With the Pilocarpine, well, we'll see how it goes. That's the best I can do—now. If the FDA changes its mind, that's something else."

Helpless feelings seemed to paralyze me. Yet I knew I had to act if we were ever to have a chance at THA. I had to persuade the FDA, or pressure it—something—to get it to act, to change its mind, to let Jane be part of the group she technically was a part of anyway.

I began to think of what I could do, to plan—and to act. Sitting out there in California, away from my files and office telephone and typewriter, I felt particularly alone and weak. Yet I'd have to get people to help me, to find someone—or a number of someones—to act for me.

Certainly I'd go to the press. Perhaps enough reporters or special writers could be aroused to investigate the FDA.

I'd go to my congressmen. Maybe Senator Bradley and Senator Lautenberg would request the FDA to make an exception in Jane's case.

Then I'd appeal to prominent doctors . . . lawyer friends of mine . . . people in the communications and advertising businesses . . . executives in business . . . writers . . . Perhaps an avalanche of letters and opinion would catch the FDA's attention, yet I also knew how unstructured, how wild and untargeted it was.

I learned that Jane needed a special designation. It was called "Compassionate Investigative New Drug," or Compassionate IND for short. My case, I felt, was a strong one—that Jane had been accepted into Dr. Summers's program more than a month before the FDA called its sudden, arbitrary halt. And the reason for that was still up in the air.

For advice, I called my longtime friend, Edward J. Michelson, a journalist who had worked in Washington, D.C., for forty-five years. He had been my first editor at CBS shortwave. As he always did, Ed picked up the picture quickly. He sensed the problem and my need.

"Bureaucracies are peculiar, Woody," he said. "I'll be glad to do what I can." And he did. He became my alter ego in Washington. Ed visited congressmen's offices, made telephone calls, investigated . . . whatever needed to be done. He and I were on the phone together every day.

Instead of going directly to Senator Bill Bradley's office, I called Jane's friend and classmate, Margaret Goheen, wife of the former president of Princeton University. She, I was sure, was a good friend of Bill Bradley's. If anyone could get through to Bradley, she could. In the past, I'd tried to touch base with Bradley but always found myself corresponding with an uninterested staff member. But Margaret, I was sure, could get right to the senator.

As I knew she would, Margaret quickly agreed to help. Besides, she had questions of her own about the FDA. She said she would get in touch with Bill Bradley right away.

"Now—how is Jane?" she asked. "And how are you?"

"Jane is her usual plucky self," I said. "She's doing everything I ask of her. We see the doctor every day. She's gone through tests that show she's a pretty sick girl." I told her that Jane also had Parkinson's and had suffered a number of tiny strokes and an infarction in her brain stem.

"I'm okay," I went on. "But if we can just win this fight against the FDA I'll feel a lot better."

I felt I should touch base again with Dr. Leon Thal, Jane's former neurologist at Albert Einstein College of Medicine in the Bronx. Now Dr. Thal was chief of neurology at the San Diego Veterans' Hospital. I thanked him again for all his help, and for giving Jane a referral to Dr. Summers. I reminded him that he had said there just might be some value in THA, but that it should be studied by more researchers. I recalled to him that he had encouraged me to take Jane to Dr. Summers, if I could, but not to expect too much. Now, I wanted his thinking about the FDA—and what I might do about THA.

"I can't understand the FDA," I went on. "Why does it allow Dr. Summers to treat forty patients—but suddenly, without any apparent reason, won't let him take on Jane as a forty-first, especially when she was accepted into his program over a month ago? It doesn't make sense."

"There has to be some cut-off in research," he explained. "Otherwise, there'd be no end, no controls."

"Well," I persisted, "I want to get a Compassionate IND designation for Jane. I want her to get THA."

"I'm afraid you won't get the Compassionate IND," he said. "The FDA is tough about such things."

"I'm going to try," I said. "I have to."

"Yes, I know you'll try, knowing you," he said, irony in his voice. "If you *do* get it, and Jane gets into the program, be sure to keep in touch with me, will you? I'd like to know how it comes out.

"But let me repeat," he went on, "the chances of Jane's improving are very slim. She's quite far along, you know. The drug doesn't stop the progress of Alzheimer's. Sometimes I think it might be easier—on her—not to fight against the odds."

"Yes, I understand," I said. "But still, I'm going to try. I'm sure—I know—Jane would want to."

Firm as I may have sounded to Dr. Thal, I really felt weak and discouraged. He was probably right. The FDA was tough. I'd not known it ever to give in, although it probably had. But I had to try. I had to.

Ed Michelson called and told me about the FDA consumer protection spokesman, David Banks, with whom he had talked the day before.

"Banks tells me that they've had trouble with Dr. Summers," Ed said. "He doesn't follow procedures. And apparently they're mad about the article in the *New England Journal of Medicine*."

"Why, I wonder?" I asked, mostly to myself. I knew why, or suspected why. "They're probably jealous."

"Maybe," Ed said. "More likely they're harassed. It's probable that they've had calls from physicians all over the country. Wanting to know more about THA. Wanting to know how they can get hold of it for their patients. When they can't have it, then there's hell to pay. Always."

"Give 'em the drug, then," I said. "The victims are going to die, anyway. Let families decide whether to use the drug."

Ed went on to tell me more about his conversation with Banks.

"He wasn't very encouraging, Wood. Apparently he knows that the 'letter' to Summers hasn't gone out yet. But he said it would definitely go out today. It spells out what Summers has to do."

Again I had that sinking feeling. I had visions of FDA directives forcing Summers to develop data over months, even a year or more—while Jane waited in vain for the help THA might give her. While the FDA insisted on its goddamned rules, Jane languished, with help for her right there.

My feelings swung from fury to despair to fury again. This wasn't good for me, I knew.

Why not call David Banks directly myself? I thought. I'd find out what I had to do to get a Compassionate IND for Jane.

When I reached Banks, I said, "I'm calling about my wife, Jane Wirsig. She was accepted as a patient by Dr.

Summers last December. That means she was a part of his program. Then a month later, when the FDA stopped Dr. Summers from taking more patients, my wife was left hanging. If THA is safe for forty other patients, why can't Dr. Summers treat my wife?"

"You don't understand," said Banks. "Dr. Summers hasn't given us the data we've asked for."

"But he says, first of all, that you haven't asked for it," I said. "And in the second place, he says he's sent it in—and it's lost there someplace."

"That's not my understanding," he said. "We don't have enough of Dr. Summers's data. We especially don't have any toxicity data—any animal studies. We have to have it if he's to go on researching THA—if we're to let more people have the drug."

"Are you sure the problem isn't something else?" I asked. "Too many people calling the FDA? Too many wanting the drug? Giving you people problems?"

Too often in such situations I get angry and speak caustically. This time, I stayed calm, but I was furious. I tried to be cool. My voice was level and, I felt, reasonable. I was trying to get to the heart of the matter—and cope with the real reason the FDA was balking.

"Mr. Banks," I went on, "what do I have to do to get a Compassionate IND for my wife? So she can have the THA drug?"

There was a pause on the line. "I'm sorry," Banks answered. "I don't think you can get it for her."

That was about as final as anything could be, I guessed. And I was in a rage. I wanted to shout, to scream at him, to inundate him with profane words. It was so unreasonable—so irrational. But I didn't swear. Instead, I spoke even more quietly.

"Well," I said, "you know that I have to try, don't you?"

"Yes," he said.

"Then that's it," I said. "I'll simply have to see what I can do."

In my mind I'd been composing a letter to send to people I thought might be willing to write . . . to help . . . to exert some pressure on the FDA.

To me, the decision was simple. Jane had already been accepted into the THA program. More than thirty-five others were already being treated. Apparently, THA was safe. So the only thing holding Jane back was procedural . . . the usual bureaucratic nightmare. I felt I was right in pushing ahead.

Although I'd campaigned for people and issues in the past, I'd never faced something like this. To me, the FDA was an unknown, amorphous group of faceless individuals who were bent on doing as they damn well pleased.

I decided to send my letter to senators, congressmen . . . to as many influential people as I could think of who might help. This is the letter:

Dear——

I urgently need your help and influence to give life back to my wife. My request, I believe, is fair and appropriate. It will not harm or inconvenience anyone. I'm asking your help in persuading the Food and Drug Administration to correct an unnecessary and arbitrary decision that will doom my wife, a victim of Alzheimer's disease, to swift decline and death. Here, as succinctly as I can, is a description of my problem and my request:

"I, Woodrow Wirsig, request that my wife, Jane D. Wirsig, be designated by the FDA as a 'Compassionate IND' to participate in Dr. William K. Summers's Alzheimer's Treatment Research Project with the drug THA. Dr. Summers has successfully been treating patients with THA for three years; a report of his work has appeared in article form in the *New England Journal of Medicine*. Mrs. Wirsig was *accepted* into Dr. Summers's program in December of 1986 and scheduled to begin treatment January 27, 1987. She was taken from her nursing home, lodging was arranged in California, airline tickets bought. Then, about a week prior to January 27, Dr. Summers received a telephone call from someone—he does not know who—from the FDA, telling him not to accept any more patients. No reasons were given, only that a letter would follow. That letter has not yet arrived in Dr. Summers's office. Mrs. Wirsig is in California now, desperately awaiting treatment that could affect the rest of her life.

"The FDA claims it has procedural and technical reasons for stopping Dr. Summers at his present forty patients. Research in THA is to be turned over to the NIH and Alzheimer's Disease and Related Disorders organization. Dr. Summers, of course, can continue treating his present forty patients.

"I am convinced, after considerable investigation, that underlying reasons for the FDA's action at this time are (1) critical editorials in the *Wall Street Journal*, and (2) jealousy, envy, political positioning, and similar attitudes not only among some officers in the FDA but also by other medical people in the U.S. There are no relevant medical or health or even procedural reasons to prevent Dr. Summers from including Mrs. Wirsig in his program. Technically, she *is already* a part of his program. But Dr. Summers is reluctant to proceed with her until he has a designation for her of Compassionate IND. This designation means 'Compassionate Investigative New Drug.'

"I therefore request an immediate designation for Mrs. Wirsig as Compassionate IND so that she may begin the treatment she entered in December—and that will enhance the rest of her life."

I have checked out THA with medical experts in New York and California. All say "there's really something to THA." Dr. Summers has kept the FDA informed about his research from the beginning. The FDA says he hasn't sent them toxicity reports. He says (1) they haven't asked for such reports but that (2) he has sent such reports to the FDA. Two factors probably lie behind the FDA's attitude: Dr. Summers uses the 'fee for service research' approach that is becoming controversial. Also, he hopes to have proprietary interest in the results of his creativity and enterprise. This annoys many in the FDA and medical field.

A substantial research project is now hurriedly being organized. Dr. Summers will be invited to participate as an advisor. They say they hope to finish the project by October, so the drug can be distributed widely. We all know that cannot possibly happen. In any case, October would be too late for Mrs. Wirsig.

To the FDA, it seems to me, there should be little or no difference between forty patients Dr. Summers is now treating and has been treating for some three years, and forty-one—which would include Mrs. Wirsig.

Mrs. Wirsig and I have lived in Princeton for thirty-five years. We reared three sons there. Jane Wirsig, a graduate cum laude from Vassar, who won all possible prizes at the Columbia Graduate School of Journalism, was Corporate Secretary of Educational Testing Service just six years ago, as well as Chairman of the Princeton Area Chamber of Commerce, one of only two women to hold that position. Now she is totally disabled.

Two and a half years ago I suffered a heart attack from the stress of caring for Mrs. Wirsig. A year later I finally had to enter her in the Princeton Nursing Home, but ever since I have fed her two meals a day, taken her for daily walks, brought her home for visits each afternoon. Now that we're in California, waiting, I am taking care of her twenty-four hours a day, and am under considerable stress as you can imagine. For these reasons, I'd appreciate your assistance as soon as possible. Thank you for your help. All good wishes.

Best regards,
Woodrow Wirsig

My son Guy offered to produce these letters on his computer. When I realized how many I planned to send, his offer was a godsend. I decided to send the letter to:

- Senator Bill Bradley. Ed Michelson had been in touch with Bradley's press relations man, John Steele. He, in turn, suggested I talk with the consumer assistance person in Bradley's Hackensack, New Jersey office, Mary Jo Wilford. Which I did. When she asked for a letter, I sent her this one.
- Senator Frank Lautenberg. Ed told me that I should send it to the attention of Chris Walsh, public affairs executive in Lautenberg's office. He suggested I mark the letter for the attention of Joy Silver.
- Congressman James Courter, from my district in New Jersey. Ed visited the office and found the Courter people—especially Courter's assistant Mack Carey—eager to be of help to me. He assigned a young woman, Beth McConnell, to investigate what might be done.
- Barton A. Cummings, former chairman of Compton Advertising, a distinguished leader in the advertising field and a longtime friend. I knew he would have Washington contacts.
- Tom Shaw, chief litigator at the prestigious law firm Breed Abbott and Morgan, a member of the Board of the Better Business Bureau, a man whom I liked and admired. Surely he would have Washington influence. Besides, Jane had once done him a favor in one of his cases.
- Dr. Eugene Friedman, a very successful New York surgeon whom I had helped become a member of the University Club. He had been active in developing medical programs for Israel. Somehow, I thought, he might have some clout.
- S. O. Shapiro, "Shap," a famous magazine circulation director with whom I had worked at *Quick* and *Look*

magazines, who always seemed to find ways to get things done, who would work hard for his friends.

- Egon Dumler, good friend and legal advisor to Jane and me, who never hesitated to fight for a good cause.
- Didi Burke, youthful wife of the chairman of Johnson & Johnson, whom, when she was a young mother, I had pictured on the cover of *Woman's Home Companion* magazine. A long shot, but I thought perhaps she might persuade her husband to bring pressure to bear on the FDA.
- Hu Pryor and Mary Scott "Scotty" Welch, good friends and former staff members of *Look*. They might have contacts somewhere in government and might be willing to write.
- Al Otten, an editorial executive of the *Wall Street Journal*'s Washington bureau and former manager of the bureau, who had been a journalism classmate of Jane's and mine at Columbia.

In talking with Al Otten on the phone, I got some additional suggestions—and some insight into the way congressmen worked.

"Woody," said Al, "you might also contact Bernard J. Dwyer, congressman from Edison, New Jersey. He's very close to several members of the House Appropriations Committee. Departments of the government listen when Appropriations Committee members talk to them. Dwyer could do a real job for you, if he wanted to.

"But—you'd better be sure to let him know you've also contacted Courter. And let Courter's office know you're contacting Dwyer's office for help. As a matter of courtesy, congressmen don't involve themselves in another's constituency—unless that representative knows about it and approves."

- Stan Rose, the influential owner and publisher of Sun Publications in Kansas City. The moment Stan got my letter, he lifted the phone and called me.

"Woody," he said, "I've already called Bob Dole's

office and spoken to Nancy Kassebaum. Now, what else can I do?"

"If they'll go to the FDA, Stan," I said, "that's great." I told him what I'd been doing, how furious I was with the FDA. I stressed that the FDA's letter still had not arrived in Dr. Summers's office. In the meantime, Jane was still sitting, waiting. . . .

"Send a letter to Nancy Kassebaum, Woody, will you?" Stan asked. "It'll help her staff go to work on the problem." I wrote to Senator Kassebaum that very day.

- Dr. James B. Dealy, Jane's brother, a distinguished roentgenologist at Massachusetts General and a professor at Tufts Medical School, whose opinion should carry weight.

- Ronald Schiller, a roving editor for the *Reader's Digest* who had written often for me at *Look* and *Woman's Home Companion.* He is a journalist who might know somebody who knows somebody who could be persuasive.

  At that moment I recalled DeWitt Wallace, founder and great editor of the *Digest* who died a few years ago. Again, I regretted his passing, for I know he'd have thrown his weight into the FDA fight for me. He had supported me in a number of my foundation efforts at the BBB.

- Richard Givens, former head of the Federal Trade Commission's office in New York. Dick is a bright, youthful lawyer with whom I had often held philosophical discussions about government's involvement in consumer affairs. Now, with a private law firm in New York, he might, I felt, still have some good contacts in Washington.

- Sara Ann Determan, wife—or former wife, I guess she is—of an executive with the Council of Better Business Bureaus in Washington. Sara Ann was a brilliant lawyer with a firm in Washington. In a conversation with her once, she had offered to be of help to me if I ever needed her. I surely needed her now.

- William Gaskill, dear friend and former chairman of the public relations firm of T. J. Ross and Associates (formerly Ivy Lee and T. J. Ross). Since Jane's illness, and his retirement, we had not been in touch. I found him living in Albuquerque, New Mexico, suffering from congestive heart failure.

"Woody," he wrote, "I've been out of touch for seven years. But I am willing to try." He enlisted the help of another retired Ross associate, living in the Washington area.

"I accept that this [congestive heart failure] will get me in the end," he said. "But until then, I'm walking every day and trying to have as much time as possible with my dear wife, Mary. . . . We celebrated our 50th wedding anniversary last week. . . ."

- Several times Ed Michelson suggested that I enlist the help of Representative Henry Waxman, of California.

"He is a senior member of the congressional delegation from California," Ed said. "He's relatively young yet something of a power in Democratic politics in the state's Southland. Waxman gets substantial attention from the L.A. *Times*' Washington bureau."

So I sent off a copy of my letter to Congressman Waxman, to the attention of Karen Nelson on Waxman's staff. I added, in the letter, all of my connections with Southern California—having worked on the L.A. *Times*, attending Occidental, my son Guy's work at the BBB.

- My brother Alan offered to help.

"Can I write our Colorado congressman?" he asked.

"Sure," I said. "I think the more letters, the more inquiries, the better."

"Then I'll write our senators," he said. "Another thing. A young woman we met over the weekend works for Senator Metzenbaum in Washington. He's interested in Alzheimer's. Should I contact her?"

"Why not?" I said. "I disagree with most everything

Metzenbaum does or says. But if he's working on Alzheimer's, he can't be all bad."

Many mornings I found myself manning the phone between feeding Jane her eggs and cereal. I could feel the stress, yet I had to go on. Underneath it all, I had a sense of floundering. There wasn't any special thrust to what I was doing. I had nothing specific to aim at. Somehow, even though all these people might go to bat for me, I had the feeling it was mushy, amorphous, slipping away. I felt I'd never get Jane into the THA program.

Still, Jane and I kept on. With regularity I gave Jane her Pilocarpine and Sinemet. We walked regularly. Most of the time she seemed cheerful. There were days when she walked gracefully, with long rhythmic strides. Other days, she would quickly lapse into the stutter steps so filled with Parkinsonian tension. Yet we kept on. And the plucky little woman never protested. She tried everything I asked of her. But we were waiting. . . .

A call from Washington came through one morning. I had difficulty identifying the caller at first. A lindrake? What, or who, was a lindrake? Then my mind must have cleared, for I heard the woman's voice saying again, "This is Lynn Drake, Dr. Lynn Drake. I'm with Senator Dole's office in Washington. He's asked me to look into Mrs. Wirsig's case. Can we talk for a few minutes?"

"We sure can," I said. "We can talk for hours if you like. I'm sorry I seemed so befuddled before. . . ."

"That's all right," she said. It was a firm voice. She seemed sure of herself, businesslike. "I have your letter to Senator Dole here. But I'd like you to tell me what this is all about. I want to know as much as I can before I go to the FDA."

So I told her everything, from my point of view. She listened, interrupting only once in a while to ask a question.

"At this point," she said, "without knowing any more about it, I can't see why Dr. Summers can't treat your wife. What's his problem?"

"He doesn't want to," I said, "until he gets this damned letter from the FDA. It's been weeks, now. Supposedly coming any day. David Banks told me it was going into the mail that day last week when I talked with him. But of course it didn't. It was a lie." I knew I sounded bitter. But that's the way I felt.

"Well, something seems to be fishy," she said. "But we'll see what goes on back here. Will you be at this telephone number most of the time, now?"

"Mornings, certainly," I said. "Late mornings and afternoons we're scheduled to see Dr. Summers."

"Oh? What's he doing?"

"He's giving Jane Pilocarpine and Sinemet," I said.

"Does it help?" she asked.

"Somewhat, I think," I said. "But I want that THA."

Without knowing precisely why, I felt much better after talking with Dr. Lynn Drake. She sounded young. But she also conveyed an ability to get to the heart of a matter. And best of all, she seemed to be willing to work at a problem to get it solved.

Soon after Dr. Drake and I had met by phone, and talked, Stan Rose called to say he had talked with Senator Kassebaum. She was personally tackling the case.

"Nancy's trying hard, Woody," he said. "And doing her best. But I think she's being buffaloed by those creeps in the FDA. They're telling her that the safety of patients is their prime priority—and they don't know how safe THA is. They tell her they can't let Dr. Summers treat more patients until they have a better idea how toxic the drug is. That, it sounds to me, is a lot of shit. I didn't tell Nancy quite that way. I don't mean that the FDA shouldn't be concerned about safety. But they should differentiate among projects. Anyway, Nancy's going to talk to them again."

Then I told him about Dr. Drake, from Senator Dole's office. Stan was interested and wanted me to be sure to let him know how she made out.

"Dole is strong," Stan said. "He is fearless. And he knows how to get things done. Besides, maybe because of his own wounds in the war, he seems very compassionate toward disabled people."

"Lynn Drake sounds great to me," I said. "She sounds like a tiger who'll stick with it until she's done the job."

One morning, Lynn—I'd been calling her Lynn for some days, now, because it was easier than constantly saying "Dr. Drake"—called to say that she felt she had found one of the problems, or at least some of the trouble.

"I'm interviewing up the ladder at the FDA," she said. "I don't want any noses to get out of joint. At least any more than they are. And there's one thing that keeps cropping up. Dr. Summers seems to be charging quite a lot for the drug and his services."

"He calls it 'fee for service,'" I said. "It's because he can't get any grants. And he simply has to have money to pay a staff large enough to do all the things the FDA requires."

"Yes—yes," she said, doubtfully. "But Mr. Wirsig, the only way the FDA can make sure patients aren't mulcted by charlatans is to prevent physicians from charging for a research drug."

"But how are doctors supposed to live—and work—if they can't get the money?" I asked. "It seems to me that if patients are willing and able to pay, they should have that choice. And chance."

"Yes," she said again, "but don't you see? The FDA has to have some method of control."

"Then," I said firmly, "the FDA ought to use some goddamned judgment."

"Don't get excited," she said. "And don't lose heart. I think we're getting somewhere. I'm only interested in getting Mrs. Wirsig into the THA program. After that, Dr. Summers can go his own way. I'll soon be talking with Dr. Katz and Dr. Leber. Then we'll see."

For her files, I sent Dr. Drake everything I could lay my hands on, including a copy of Dr. Summers's article in the

New England Journal of Medicine and copies of the *Wall Street Journal*'s series of brilliant editorials criticizing the FDA's intransigence in moving on drugs that showed promise of helping fatally ill patients.

In the mail came copies of letters to the FDA written by Dr. Eugene Friedman and Egon Dumler. Both letters were polite but hard-hitting and to the point, in effect demanding that Jane be given the Compassionate IND to undergo treatment with THA.

Shap—dear Shap—at first was nonplussed by my request for help. He couldn't think of what to do, but wanted so much to help me. Then he thought of the Anti-Defamation League, with its powerful Washington office. He wrote Nathan Perlmutter, national director. Back came a letter saying: "Dear Shap: I'm writing you from Palm Beach where we are for our annual meetings. I've discussed your letter concerning Woodrow Wirsig with Dave Brody, who will look into it. We'll keep you advised but I simply wanted you to know that we got your letter and we're acting on it."

Bart Cummings had immediately written an executive in the FDA whom he knew. . . .

Hu Pryor wrote the National Committee to Preserve SS and Medicare. . . .

Beth McConnell went directly to the legislative section of the FDA. This was the routine course for such inquiries. It was set up that way, I was sure, to keep pressures off the FDA itself.

"Mr. Wirsig," she said over the phone, "I don't think you're going to get a Compassionate IND for Mrs. Wirsig. I'll keep trying. But there seems to be too much of a principle at stake here."

"Thank you, Beth," I said. "Please—keep trying." Somehow, I felt more discouraged than ever. I felt that my moods were swinging up and down like a yo-yo, much too wildly to be comfortable—or good for me, I was sure.

While I was negotiating with these Washington offices,

I felt I had to keep up Dr. Summers's morale. Initially, after his staff had received the first phone call from the FDA, he was so angry he was ready to stop all THA research. I persuaded him to keep on—not to lose all that he had achieved. I urged him to realize that his job was medical and neurological. He shouldn't be trying to be a public relations executive, a lawyer, and a businessman, too.

At one point, Dr. Summers was ready to fly back to Washington to hold a press conference.

"I'll blast the damned roof off the FDA," he snorted.

I offered to find him a place at the National Press Club to hold such a press conference. But I also suggested that he might think about it awhile. The next day I told him that such a press conference would generate a great deal of heat—and probably not very much light. In the end, I said, it would probably harm his work rather than help it.

Dr. Summers himself has made some errors in judgment—and probably some errors in commission. A letter from the editor of the *New England Journal of Medicine*, Arnold S. Relman, M.D., following publication of Dr. Summers's article, asked (1) if Solo Research, Inc., was a for-profit tax-paying corporation, and (2) whether Dr. Summers received any economic benefits from the income generated by the corporation. And if the answers were yes, why hadn't Dr. Summers provided this information "in accordance with our stated policy before we arranged for publication of your recent paper?"

In answering the letter, Dr. Summers said that he had no sense of a conflict of interest in the matter. Attempts to obtain funding by more traditional means, he explained, had failed despite continued apparent success with THA. Solo Research, he said, was initiated at the request of an accountant for the express purpose of being more ethical about preventing co-mingling of research funds and private medical corporation income. Solo Research, he pointed out, was initiated after the initial submission of the manuscript. Finally, he said, attempts to review the fee-for-service model and the pamphlet just prior to publication of the article were made in a timely fashion with perceived authorities.

"I apologize," said Dr. Summers in his letter, "for any inconvenience and embarrassment that may have occurred. I would like to reassure you that any such embarrassment was certainly not my intent."

It was becoming clearer to me that Dr. Summers wanted to be perceived as a traditional medical man, interested in helping the sick. But he also was interested in money. Dr. Summers was interested in money not only for his research staff and office costs but also, in the long run, as a substantial reward for his creativity and work. He told me that he had a patent attorney working on ways of establishing some proprietary interest in THA, which could not be patented. He was trying, he said, to get a drug company to work with him in establishing some kind of exclusivity over the drug while funding his ongoing treatment of patients. In other words, Dr. Summers may well have used his article in the *New England Journal of Medicine* to promote his privately owned fee-for-service research program, while trying to get some kind of proprietary interest in THA, which he thought someday soon could be a $500 million market.

It was obvious to me that the FDA, privately angry about Dr. Summers's efforts to profit by THA, was using technical questions about toxicity and procedures, and so on, to hamper Dr. Summers's treatment of patients with THA.

And Jane was caught in the middle.

Winter nights in Los Angeles can be uncomfortably cold. Although I had an electric blanket for Jane, I worried that it might be too hot or too cold. How could I know? Since she couldn't tell me and had been coughing during the last few weeks, I worried more than ever. I found myself waking up at 2 A.M. or so to feel whether Jane was too warm or too cold.

Reluctantly, because such things never seemed to work

well for me, I decided to hire a nurse to help me care for Jane. For once I was lucky. A nursing services agency, recommended to me by the beauty parlor girl who fixed Jane's hair each week, sent me a young woman, Lisa Vasquez, who had been trained as a nurse's aide. She was young, married, the mother of a three-year-old boy—and turned out to be superb. She was that rare person, someone with initiative who cared about her work and her patient. Almost at once I felt comfortable in turning over to her Jane's bathing, toileting, clothing, and feeding. She toileted Jane every hour and a half on the dot—and kept records, took Jane's blood pressure regularly, and found other things to do for us around the house.

In some ways, Jane was thriving. Her weight was holding despite—or maybe because of—the baby food I'd brought in to provide the pureed food she required. With the Pilocarpine and Sinemet, she was walking better than she had some weeks before at the nursing home in Princeton. More than anything else, however, she seemed to be trying to talk more. She was smiling, reacting to conversation and questions.

As for my campaign to persuade the FDA, I still felt it was a floundering, mixed-up, unstructured activity without a sharp focus. I was becoming resigned to taking Jane home without the THA. I would keep trying, but . . .

I never heard from Congressman Dwyer. Senator Lautenberg's office sent me a note saying that they were contacting the legislative section of the FDA—and enclosed a newspaper article telling me about Alzheimer's disease. Senator Bradley's office let me know that they, too, were contacting the legislative section of the FDA and we should be hearing from them. I couldn't be sure, of course, but I had the feeling that both senators' staff people would get bogged down in the FDA's legislative section and probably would never be heard from again.

No word came from Sara Ann Determan or Didi Burke. Perhaps I never reached Sara Ann; perhaps she had forgotten who I was. And I really couldn't expect Didi and her husband to do anything. Johnson & Johnson couldn't get involved in a single case of this kind, not if it expected to have scrupulous relations with the FDA for its multibillion-dollar drug company. Of course, even so, they *could* have tried. At least, it would have been nice to hear from them.

If anything were to happen—if, by chance, we had any success—it seemed to me it would come from the work of Dr. Lynn Drake. I had to admire Dr. Drake. She had stamina. Apparently the people she talked with at the FDA were persuasive about Dr. Summers. She tended, in our discussions about Dr. Summers, to side with the FDA. At the same time, she was definitely working to get a reversal for Jane so she could receive the THA drug.

"At this point," Dr. Drake said to me, laughing a bit, "I couldn't care less about Dr. Summers's troubles with the FDA. But I do want him to include Jane in the group receiving THA. I think—I really think—we may be getting somewhere. What I'm doing is preparing a report on the situation for Senator Dole and his associate, Sheila Burke. Eventually, they will talk with the FDA commissioner.

"Incidentally," she added, "every one of those letters you've asked people to write? Well, they help. Every one of them has helped."

For some reason, at that moment, I felt more discouraged than ever. A disorganized group of letters, expressing opinions of the writers? How could they possibly persuade that intransigent bunch of bastards in the FDA?

Several times Dr. Drake called Dr. Summers to check on details of his program. He felt she was helpful and cooperative and began to trust her. She asked him only for facts and avoided any argument over policies.

To my surprise, our situation began to change the day after the Presidents Day holiday, February 16. First, Dr. Summers received the long-awaited letter from the FDA. When I saw him he was so angry I could see that he was ready to blow up.

"I'm going to fight them on every point," he declared. "They're wrong. Damned wrong. Or misinformed on just about every point."

A second letter arrived that day from the FDA, which Dr. Summers hadn't seen when we talked. To this day I haven't seen it, either. But I have a copy of the "first" letter, a big, nine-page, single-spaced official letter setting out what the FDA demanded of Summers.

To me, the FDA letter was offensive from beginning to end. It took the tone of a lofty school principal spanking a naughty student. The letter criticized Dr. Summers's manufacturing and controls. It complained that he was moving ahead before appropriate animal toxicity studies were done. It criticized his clinical procedures. It accused him of misusing his IND for commercial purposes. It made additional requests for full reports. It made negative comments on his proposal for future investigations, complaining that he initiated his work on THA as an academic sponsor-investigator—but then became a commercial drug developer, which required different procedures. In summary, the letter said Dr. Summers could increase the number of his patients to forty-five (which would make room for Jane), but not until he had complied with all of the FDA demands. And the FDA stipulated that Dr. Summers could not charge any patient for THA. Neither could he charge more than the usual office fee charged by doctors generally in the Los Angeles area.

In other words, he would have to buy the THA out of his own pocket (it was running about $40,000 a year for all his patients) and support a staff to conduct the research and keep the records, all out of his own pocket.

The FDA was being awfully tough and arrogant, it seemed to me. Were they this demanding of other researchers? I doubted that they made such demands of others. They seemed to be punishing Dr. Summers.

The next day, February 18, I talked again with Dr. Lynn Drake. Apparently she knew what the "second" letter to Dr. Summers contained.

"I've just talked with Dr. Summers," she said, "and he says he is 'going to enroll you guys.'"

That was news to me. Encouraging—but I had to wait until I could speak with Dr. Summers himself.

On the morning of February 19 came the memorable call from Washington. It was 6 A.M., California time—and the call woke me from the first good sleep I'd had since coming there. The voice, clear and authoritative, came over the line:

"Mr. Wirsig?"

"Yes. This is he."

"This is Frank Young, commissioner of the FDA. Can you hear me all right? I'm calling from my car phone . . ."

He was calling to tell me what I had suspected from my talk with Dr. Drake the day before. The way had been cleared for Dr. Summers to increase the number of his patients on THA to forty-five, which would include Jane.

I was so glad, so overwhelmingly glad. Jane now would have a chance at a drug that could help her think more like herself, walk more as she used to, recognize her family and friends.

That night, Senator Nancy Kassebaum, who must have heard that Commissioner Young had told me Jane could get THA, called me from Washington to wish Jane good luck in her treatment.

After my talk with Senator Kassebaum, I sat down to write a letter to all those who had been of help to Jane and me in this matter. It had to be duplicated, to get out as soon as possible, but I wanted to let everyone know that Jane had won. My letter was dated February 20:

My heartfelt thanks for the help I asked of you to get Food and Drug Administration approval for Jane Wirsig to be treated with the drug THA. I hope to thank you better in person as soon as possible.

Jane has won.

She begins her treatment Monday, February 23.

This four-week battle culminated yesterday morning at 6 A.M. California time. A call from Washington, D.C., woke me from the first good sleep I've had since coming here. A voice, clear and authoritative, came over the line:

"Mr. Wirsig? This is Frank Young, Commissioner of the FDA. Can you hear me all right? I'm calling from my car phone. . . ."

He was calling to tell me the way had been cleared for Dr. William K. Summers to increase the number of his patients on THA to 45, which would include Jane. Dr. Young assured me he was impressed with Dr. Summers's work. As quickly as possible, he said, he was pushing for studies at the National Institute of Aging. These would replicate Dr. Summers's work so that the drug could be made available to millions of Alzheimer's disease victims as soon as possible.

I won't burden you with details of these last four weeks. The fight was bitter and disheartening, filled with statements and denials, changes of mind, envy and probably the worst of all bureaucratic intransigence.

You would want to know, I think, that Senator Bob Dole's staff members, Dr. Lynn Drake and Sheila Burke, patiently and persistently pushed Jane's case right up to the point where Senator Dole could step in and discuss the issue reasonably with Frank Young. Commissioner Young, in our conversation, referred to "my good friend Bob Dole." I was impressed with Senator Dole's compassion, his willingness to take time and make the effort to be interested in Jane's case.

Senator Nancy Kassebaum added her personal weight. She called me last evening to wish Jane good luck in her treatment. I took the opportunity to encourage her in her proposed 'affidavit' program to enable the terminally ill to benefit from experimental drugs early rather than too late.

Frank Courter's staff member, Beth McConnell, also pitched in. To me, it was most important to have Dr. Lynn Drake tell me that every letter, every phone call, every effort by anyone to persuade the FDA in this case would help.

So—I'm sure that *every* effort played its part in giving Jane her chance.

I wish I could say I'm happy and excited over the victory, but I'm not. I'm disheartened at so much time and effort of so many good people in a battle that never should have had to be waged. There are so many millions out there who need this help—and it will be years and years yet before they get it. . . .

For Jane and for me, bless you.

17

Jane on THA: Does It Help?

Now the test. No more barriers. Jane could begin getting THA. What would happen? Were we too late? I wondered. Would it—could it—be possible for Jane to have a year, even two years, more of conscious happiness? I felt as if we were starting our last adventure together.

It was Friday, February 20, 1987, in Dr. Summers' office in Arcadia, California.

"Stop the Pilocarpine for Jane right away," Dr. Summers told me. "Her system must be completely free of Pilocarpine before we start THA on Monday."

"Wouldn't it be best," I asked, thinking of the side effects from THA, "if Jane went into a hospital for the first few weeks of this treatment?"

Dr. Summers nodded. "It's the best way. We can know we control the dosage. We can monitor her reactions. It's easier for me to see her every day." The side effects of THA didn't affect every patient, of course, nor were they very serious: some nausea, sweating, enzyme changes in the liver, which disappeared when THA was stopped.

We discussed which hospital might be better for her, the big, well-known Huntington Memorial or Las Encinas, an old but beautiful psychiatric hospital, both in Pasadena. I leaned toward the Huntington. Technically, I felt, it might be better. But for Jane's purposes, Dr. Summers leaned toward Las Encinas.

"One more thing," Dr. Summers said. "You go into the Huntington, you're stuck with the whole bill, no matter what. In Las Encinas, I'll also be treating Jane for her mood disorder and strokes. That way Medicare will pick up at least some of the costs. If costs are important to you, that is."

"Of course," I said. "Who wouldn't think of them? But we can handle anything they throw at us. I'm most concerned that Jane get what she needs."

On Monday, Jane began taking the THA, beginning with a 50-milligram dose once a day. Tuesday afternoon we entered her into Las Encinas Hospital. Through it all Jane was calm and poised, a little smile on her face and complete awareness shining out of her eyes. She looked as if she were sharing a joke with us.

At the hospital, I was immediately informed that Jane must have a special duty nurse—three special duty nurses on three shifts, around the clock. That meant I'd have to teach two nurses how to feed Jane. Then I learned that the hospital even rotated the special duty nurses, meaning I'd have to teach more nurses how to feed Jane. Several days passed this way before I learned that I could put my foot down and insist that Jane have the same special nurse for each shift.

Why, I asked myself, do these institutions keep rotating aides and nurses? The Princeton Nursing Home did the same—and it drove me up the wall. None of the aides really came to know a patient, her habits, her needs, even her clothing. They knew a little about everybody—and nothing important about anybody. It was done for the benefit of the hospital, I concluded—certainly not for the benefit of the patient.

Dr. Summers's plan was to increase the THA dosage for Jane steadily so that by the end of the week she could be up to the maximum dose of 200 milligrams a day.

We ran into bad luck—again. At the end of the second day, one of the special nurses reported that Jane had thrown up. Another special said, "No, Jane has not thrown up." Then neither could—or would—be sure.

Dr. Summers was as indignant as I was.

"Now we'll have to start all over with the dosage," he said. "We have to know what she can—and can't—tolerate."

That meant, probably, another week in the hospital. While I could handle the expense, which would be astronomical, I was sure, I didn't want to be made a fool of, either. For the hospital to have special nurses who couldn't remember whether Jane did—or did not—throw up was, to me, unpardonably nonprofessional.

Nagging thoughts about matters at home bothered me, too. After all, we'd been away about five weeks—when I'd planned for only twenty-one days. Bills certainly were piling up. Checks were coming in that had to be deposited. More important, all my income tax materials were there. I had to work on them now if I were to get it all in to my accountant on time. That Thursday, I flew home and managed to do everything that needed doing, including sorting through what seemed to be tons of mail. I got to the bank, picked up my tax data, notified the police, the post office, and paper deliveries again, and flew back to Los Angeles on Monday.

At the hospital, Jane had been to one of the beauty parlors—and looked beautiful to me. After kissing her in bunches, I took her for a short walk. It seemed to me, wishful thinking or not, that she walked better. And she had been eating well, too, the nurses said. Once in a while she would surprise me by responding coherently to something I said or asked.

Not long after I came back, and out of the blue, she looked at me with smiling eyes and said, "I love you."

At that, so many troubles seemed to float away. To have Jane conscious of what she was saying, and to say to me, "I love you," was worth all the turmoil, all the worry.

As medication for Jane was increased, almost day by day, I watched her closely. Was she understanding me better? Could I detect more talking? Were some of her utterances clearer? How was she walking? Each day I looked for change, some evidence that Jane was benefiting from the THA. At times I thought I saw some improvement. At other times, none.

I tried to be at the hospital often—at mealtimes especially, to make sure the special nurses fed Jane slowly enough so she wouldn't throw up. At the time, we all thought her stomach upsets came from the THA. If I'd read more, I'd have known that it probably was the Sinemet that caused her to throw up. I found that I had to monitor the medication, too. Several times I found the medication nurse giving Jane the wrong amount—or giving the medicine more than an hour before the set time, or more than an hour later.

Although Jane was having formal physical therapy each day, I wanted to walk her myself, too, to mark any improvement. We walked inside the hospital, sometimes outside in the formal gardens. Most of the time Jane walked in slow, short steps culminating a few moments later in a flutter of stutter steps. We'd stop, wait a few moments, resting, then start again. And again she would walk slowly for a little while before breaking into the rapid stutter steps.

Dr. Summers thought Jane was doing nicely. He kept complimenting her on walking, on her responsiveness to him as he talked. I couldn't see it, myself, and began to wonder if he were conning me. I told myself that I couldn't have expected Jane to be better. Any hopes I had were only fooling myself, I thought. Still, I hoped. And for all my discouragement, I decided we would go through with the whole process.

One afternoon, Dr. Summers and I stood together watching a nurse walk Jane down the hall from her room.

"Jane," Dr. Summers said, almost musingly, "is so near the end of her illness that it would be a crime to give her a placebo."

Startled, I took several seconds to follow his thinking. At the time, I concluded, he was thinking about his requirement eventually to put Jane on a placebo as part of the rules of the research. Then I remembered how vigorously Dr. Summers had complained about some aspects of pure science. How sad, he had said, when a drug obviously helps a dying patient, to be forced to withdraw that drug for a while merely to go through the motions of a placebo.

In the back of my mind, I realized, he may have been trying to tell me something about Jane—to prepare me, as it were. If he was referring to the possibility of her death soon, I refused to think about it and put it out of my mind. I knew that it was going to be hard for me to handle. I thought again how much easier it would be, for me, if I went first.

We finally scheduled our flight home to Princeton on Wednesday, March 18—almost two months after we had left. I'd made arrangements by mail to enter Jane back into the Princeton Nursing Home. I admitted to myself I'd hoped to be able to bring her home and, with help, keep her here. But I soon realized that just wouldn't work.

Since we would be arriving from the airport after 10 P.M., I asked the nursing home to have a wheelchair at the entrance.

Again, we were flying first class on United. Dinner was as elegant as they could make it, from fine linens and several wines to dessert. I chose a rare roast beef entrée for Jane, for that was always her favorite. I cut up her salad into tiny pieces. I cut and tore the meat into bits. I felt I was prepared to feed her, even though she had been getting pureed food.

To my surprise, and delight, Jane slowly . . . tentatively, at first . . . began to pick up the fork herself. I waited and watched her, ready to help. But she knew what she wanted to do. She took a forkful of salad, her hand trembling slightly, and brought it toward her mouth. In her first try, she jammed the fork into her chin. Again, she tried—and hit her cheek. Just as I was about to help her, she managed to put the fork in her mouth.

I sat back to watch, and perhaps help. But slowly, haltingly, Jane ate that whole dinner by herself. I was so happy and proud of her I could burst—and I was crying, too, over the whole sad, desperate, inevitable tragedy.

Jane was feeding herself—for the first time in two years.

Those first few weeks at home again became a blur of problems for me. Jane, it seemed to me, was scheduled to get a multitude of medications, yet the nursing home insisted on getting all the medications through its own pharmacy. The law, they said.

Was there a gap in giving Jane her medicines? I think so, but I couldn't get the facts.

I finally persuaded the nursing home to take the PhosChol I'd brought back—a refined, concentrated lecithin that Dr. Summers required Jane to receive. Otherwise, he said—if I recall what he said correctly—the THA would cannibalize brain cells. The nursing home took my supply of THA because there was no other source for it.

During the day, Jane was to have PhosChol, Theragram M., Sinemet four times a day, Fiberol, Amantadine, Trental, THA, baby aspirin, Norproamine, and Ritalin. She was throwing up frequently and suddenly failed to walk nearly as well as she had been walking at Las Encinas.

More than a week went by before I realized that the nursing home was not following Dr. Summers' prescriptions. During the day, Jane was sleeping so soundly in her wheelchair I thought she might be in a coma. Waking her for feeding, or taking a walk, was difficult. Too difficult. I almost had to slap her on her cheeks to get her awake. Worry kept me on edge all day, and I was sleeping fitfully at night. Was she so lethargic because of the mood medications?

"We're not giving her the Ritalin," said a nurse. "Dr. Julio won't allow it."

At that I felt a sudden rage again. What arrogance! Dr. Julio was one of four physicians who served the patients at the nursing home. By law, a patient selected one of them—who then was responsible for health routines and medication for that patient.

What right had Dr. Julio to deny Dr. Summers's prescription for Jane? On the other hand, I realized it wasn't the drug that was making her asleep. Not knowing anything about Ritalin, I had thought perhaps it had a sedative effect.

When I talked with Dr. Julio, he said only that he felt Ritalin was not indicated, that it was a strong drug and he would not prescribe it for Jane.

"Of course," he said, "you can go to another physician if you wish."

Not until I discussed Ritalin with Dr. David Fulmer did I learn that Ritalin, regarded as a fine, old drug, was an amphetamine and highly desired by street drug dealers.

"I wouldn't prescribe it," said Dr. Fulmer. "Not because it isn't a good drug. It is good. But the narcotics officials in New Jersey just make it too difficult for physicians to use. I'd have to go through a long, elaborate routine of proof that Jane needed it, and even then I'd have trouble keeping the narcotics agents from trying to lock me up."

My dear little wife, I realized, was not getting medication for her mood disorder . . . a disorder, Dr. Summers had said, a number of times, "that is something we could do something about."

I checked back on the bottles of drugs I'd taken home

with me from Las Encinas. Sure enough, one large bottle contained enough Ritalin to medicate Jane for months.

Should I give Jane the Ritalin myself? I had the opportunity, for now I'd been able to get Jane into a private room at the nursing home. I could have privacy with her.

The temptation was great . . . is great. I haven't done it. Too many visions of news stories about spouses who harmed rather than helped their loved ones with medications they didn't understand. Still, I notice that Jane is not smiling at me and at other people as much as she did before we went to California. If she is still suffering from that mood disorder—and I suspect by mood disorder Dr. Summers means some variation of depression—then I have to find some way of getting help for her.

I still might give Jane the Ritalin myself.

For weeks I was sad and frantic at the rate Jane was throwing up her food and the medications. A stroke victim, I learned, tends to aspirate—to suck vomit back into the lungs. I watched Jane cough, then throw up, then gasp for air, sucking air—and probably vomit—back into her lungs. I couldn't stand it and wanted to give up all the new medication. Everything seemed to be going haywire. I knew she wasn't keeping enough food down to maintain her weight. She was losing much of the medication. I was simply frantic.

In a talk with Dr. Fulmer, I asked him about Sinemet and other medications—and the vomiting.

"It's the Sinemet that's giving her the biggest trouble," he said. "We've tried to tackle that problem by breaking each Sinemet pill in half—and giving it six times a day instead of three."

That same day I talked with Dr. Julio and the nurses. They agreed to try that way of giving Jane the Sinemet.

The result seemed almost a miracle. Jane stopped throwing up and seemed better in every way. I found her much less lethargic and more aware of everything around her. She began to smile at me again when I came to be with her. Her walking began to improve immediately.

Several months after our return from California, after we had finally balanced the THA and Sinemet for Jane, I reached some conclusions about THA and what we'd been putting Jane through. Many times, as I sat helping Jane cope with throwing up her meals, sick at heart, yearning so to suffer myself instead of her, I'd vowed to stop the entire experiment and let Jane be in peace for the rest of her days. Yet somehow I had persisted. Jane, love her, was plucky enough to keep trying with me. Never once did she complain or try to refuse to do anything we asked. Now I was evaluating what we had done . . . and where we stood.

On balance, I felt, Jane had improved in almost every way. She was back about where she was some two years ago—in talking, in walking, in awareness of what went on around her. Knowing that THA did not, could not, stop the progress of Alzheimer's disease, I realized that the medication seemed to be doing what it was supposed to do: help Jane have a little more time to live a little more normally.

Now Jane smiles at me and gives me bunches of kisses, as we have kissed for forty-five years. As we begin our walks, I feel her whole body tense and tight, ready to start off with stutter steps. Yet when I begin counting rhythmically, one—two—three— four—ready, let's go, her body suddenly relaxes and she moves off with me in steady, regular steps.

I've begun taking her for rides in the car—just rides around the familiar places in Princeton. Recently I drove out to Educational Testing Service for her to see the place where she worked for so many pleasant years. As we rode down the highway which was her route when she drove herself, I told her:

"Darling—this is the way you used to go to work in the

morning. And it's the way you came home to cook dinner for both of us."

At that moment, I turned to look at her. She was watching me with a big smile, her eyes wide open and weeping, in almost total recognition, it seemed to me, of fond memories and sadness that it was over and never to be recaptured.

The other day, as we were riding along Nassau Street, Jane reached over to take my hand in hers. She held it until we returned to the nursing home. She hadn't done that in several years.

Jane will probably not benefit from the cure that surely will be discovered for Alzheimer's disease eventually. It probably will be too late for her. But it's possible that it could come in time to help. And as long as it's possible, I have hope.

Our knowledge about Alzheimer's and Parkinson's diseases seems to be expanding at an exponential rate. Despite the panic over AIDS, a great amount of research goes on in many laboratories to find some preventive, some cure, for Alzheimer's and Parkinson's:

- Dr. Abraham Fisher, of the Israeli Institute of Biological Research, has designed a new drug that, Dr. Summers tells me, is better than THA in supplying the brain with a way to keep its supply of the neurotransmitter acetylcholine. He has tested it only on animals, thus far. When he's ready for human beings, I'm ready to fly with Jane to Israel.
- Four groups of researchers have discovered a specific gene that contributes to a brain-tissue abnormality characteristic of Alzheimer's. A fifth group has discovered a genetic "marker" linked to Alzheimer's.
- A protein has been discovered in the spinal fluid of Alzheimer's victims that is not present in healthy persons— which at least will assist in diagnosis of Alzheimer's.
- Surgeons in Europe have operated to insert brain tissue

from fetuses into the brains of Alzheimer's patients, with some indication of success.

- Surgeons in Mexico and the United States have begun to transplant tissue from the adrenal glands into the brains of Parkinson's victims, with good results, they say. Some surgeons believe that implanting fetal tissue will provide even better results.

- For a while, researchers discarded the theory that aluminum causes Alzheimer's, believing it couldn't pass the blood-brain barrier. Now, however, it has been discovered that aluminum inhaled through the noses of rabbits can penetrate the brain through the olfactory nerves.

- The brain may even, at times, outsmart itself by hastening Alzheimer's progress through its own functioning. This theory holds that the onset of Alzheimer's causes the brain to increase metabolic activity to create new nerve connections to take over functions of the nerve cells that have died. This, however, may increase the chances that the cells involved may become diseased. Cells that sprout new nerve fibers have a higher metabolic rate. The regenerative activity, known as neuroplasticity, may become an agent of the disease itself. Since younger people have greater neuroplasticity than older people, the increased metabolic activity in the brain would accelerate the dementia of patients with early onset of Alzheimer's.

- Nimodipine, a drug that some researchers have used to improve blood flow in elderly stroke patients' brains, has been tested on rabbits. When aging rabbits were given the drug, they learned given tasks as quickly as younger rabbits. The drug inhibits calcium flow to the brain. The drug is now undergoing tests among Alzheimer's patients to see whether it will improve their memories.

- Some experts are urging Parkinson's victims to undergo electroconvulsive therapy—ECT, as it's called, before submitting to implants of fetal tissue. Patients who did showed significant neurological improvement—along with improvement in the depression that coexisted with the disease.

- Scientists report that they have resuscitated dying nerve cells in laboratory rats by implanting genetically altered cells into the animals' brains. After two weeks, rats implanted with the tissue containing nerve growth factor retained 92 percent of damaged cells, while rats that did not receive the tissue retained only 49 percent.
- Scientists are linking Alzheimer's disease to head injuries. Studies in England show that nerve tangles and proteins in the nerve tangles previously associated with Alzheimer's also appeared in the brains of persons who had suffered head injuries.
- Senator Nancy Kassebaum and the *Wall Street Journal* are campaigning to change the Food and Drug Administration's rules on drugs that can help terminal patients. They believe that experimental drugs that have not yet met the FDA's standards for approval should be made available to the families of terminal patients, who would then decide whether to risk using such drugs.

These are only a few of the developments that may make life easier for Alzheimer's and Parkinson's victims—and their loved ones. The challenge is not the same as such challenges as flying to the moon. We cannot expect breakthroughs simply by throwing money at researching these diseases. Under President Nixon we tried that with cancer and, thus far, it hasn't worked. Answers to the Alzheimer's and Parkinson's challenges will come through the creative insights of scientists who see relationships between things that others do not see—and who live and work in an environment conducive to creative achievement.

If, as probable, some of these answers are too late to save Jane, surely the knowledge will emerge in time to save our sons, if they should fall victims . . . and their children . . . and the millions of others who will be saved for active, healthy, and happy lives.

18

"You Are My Sunshine . . ."

Near the end of her first year on THA, Jane was asked to participate in a double-blind test of her response to the drug.

I was dubious. Why now, I wondered? So vividly I remembered Dr. Summers saying, "Jane is so near the end of her illness that it would be a crime to give her a placebo."

Again, I debated with myself. Would this upset her? Could she continue to walk? Might she slip into comalike periods? Would she, could she, eat properly? Might she choke on her food?

Why, I thought, should she risk all these possibilities, or worse, at this point in her illness?

Still, I wanted to help Dr. Summers try to conform to the FDA's procedures. So I agreed that we'd participate in the double-blind test. We had to, of course, or lose Dr. Summers's care . . . and THA.

About the time the test was to start, I read that Lawrenceville Nursing Home was establishing an Alzheimer's wing. An activities director, especially trained for Alzheimer's patients, would be in charge of such activities as dancing, marching to music, coloring, practice in talking, games—even mere participatory observation.

Just what I've been looking for, I thought—sorrowful that it couldn't have come eight years earlier. I called to find out more about the nursing home's plans. I was pleased to find even more values of the kind I sought. Aides would not be rotated but would stay in the Alzheimer's wing so they could know the special needs of patients. Nurses would not be rotated, but would stay in the wing. Doctors and consultants knowledgeable about Alzheimer's would readily be on call.

In the midst of my enthusiasm came periods of agonizing . . . again. If I were to move Jane, would I be entering her into a worse situation? At least now, in the Princeton Nursing Home, there were a few aides who seemed to care. A few nurses seemed thoughtful. A few visitors got Jane to smile and respond to questions. Would I be taking her away from these people only to plunge her into a new environment that would be more confusing?

Again, I reviewed everything, point by point. At the Princeton Nursing Home, activities people cared nothing about Jane. They geared their activities to the elderly who could walk, or propel their own wheelchairs, whose minds were relatively clear. Although Jane had a private room, her bed was pushed up against the old-fashioned ventilating system. Often I'd come into her room to find her perspiring—or shivering. She always seemed to be in wet diapers, needing a change of clothing.

Finally, I decided to move her. The new place couldn't be any worse in all the things that mattered to me. So I interviewed Ronnie Bregenzer, the head nurse, and the administrator, Frank Puzio—and filled out the application forms.

"We don't know when we'll have a bed ready," Mrs.

Bregenzer said. "But when one opens in the Alzheimer's wing, we'll want Jane to enter immediately.

Right off, I liked everyone I talked to. First of all, the Lawrenceville Nursing Home is in an attractive section of Lawrenceville, a small town only a few miles from Princeton. It's famous, for the most part, for the excellent Lawrenceville School, formerly for boys but now coeducational.

The nursing home is a one-level, low-lying building built especially to be a nursing home, essentially in a square surrounding a large courtyard. I noticed immediately that the heating-cooling units in the rooms were modern and constantly controlled by thermostat.

The dining room was large and attractive, with flowers on the tables and holiday decorations on the walls.

But best of all, I noted the attitudes of the staff. Everyone was smiling, saying hello to everyone, making caring inquiries . . . as if they were all a big, happy family.

So I faced the next question: Should I move Jane immediately and carry out the double-blind study in the new facility? Or wait until after the double-blind study to move her?

I decided to wait until after the double-blind test—if only because I felt that the specific nurses in charge at the Princeton Nursing Home would handle the study with some knowledge of Jane.

None of us, of course, knew in which period Jane would take the placebo and which the real THA. Measurements would involve blood tests, EKGs, urine samples—as well as a complex battery of psychometric questions and evaluations. We asked a medical student, who worked as one of the activities personnel, to carry out the psychometric part. I made it clear that Jane could not respond to verbal questions and that much of her examination would have to be based on observation.

So the double-blind test period of six weeks began.

First, Jane would be receiving one specific batch of the

drug (or placebo) for three weeks. Then, for a second three-week period, she would use another batch of THA (or placebo). Only Dr. Summer's assistant would know which period was which.

Within days after the test period began I felt sure I knew which period was the placebo. Within hours I noticed the change in Jane's walking. She began walking and standing at such an angle that I had to hold her upright every moment. She had no rhythm in her steps. She began walking in stutter steps. Her eyes were closed most of the time. She seemed to recede into her own mind and be unaware of what went on around her. Listless, unresponsive to my kisses, Jane failed to respond to me when I visited her. Soon she began to choke more frequently on her food.

I couldn't wait for those first three weeks to end.

Within a day or so after beginning the next batch of THA (or placebo), Jane straightened up in her walk. Sparkle and light came back into her eyes. She began to talk—or try to talk—as if inside her mind she knew precisely what she wanted to say. She smiled more frequently. When I approached, she held up her face to be kissed. Again, she seemed aware of what was going on about her.

All the blood tests, EKGs, and other tests, along with the results of the psychometric tests, were sent to Dr. Summers in California without my seeing them or knowing in any way what they indicated.

But I wrote Dr. Summers: "I don't know which period was the placebo and which was the real THA. But I would bet my bottom dollar that the first three weeks were the placebo period . . . and the second three weeks were the real THA. . . ."

A few weeks later, I received a report from Dr. Summers. It said:

Re: JANE WIRSIG ENTERING PHASE 3 STUDY: I am delighted and pleased to say that Jane has been offered a position in Phase 3 of the study. As you noted in your letter, she was indeed on placebo the first three weeks and the second three weeks was on THA in the usual dosage. As you may also know, I was deeply concerned that the severity of Jane's problem was so great that it might be difficult to demonstrate THA effect in her. So, once again, I am extremely pleased. . . ."

In another letter, obviously written for the FDA file, Dr. Summers said

"We are happy to inform you that Jane D. Wirsig has shown significant improvement on THA versus placebo. As such, this letter is an invitation to participate in Phase III of the oral protocol. This is a long-term study—using in the first year placebo one out of 12 months and THA in optimal dose 11 out of 12 months. The month of placebo will be picked randomly by the research team. After the first, placebo will not be used. Please have the following tests done monthly:
 1. CBC with reticulocyte and platelet count.
 2. Prothrombin time.
 3. SMA 18 with liver function tests.
 4. Serum THA level taken 4 hours after the last dose of THA.
 5. Electrocardiogram.

About the time Jane began her double-blind study, the FDA with Warner-Lambert and the National Institute for Aging began a large three-hundred-patient test of THA to see if they could replicate Dr. Summers's findings. Then, a few weeks later, with great fanfare, the FDA announced that the test had suddenly been halted. Eight out of the first forty being tested had shown some cell changes in the liver. The *New York Times* erroneously used the term "liver damage" even though, a few days previously, in the science section, a Warner-Lambert spokesman had said the cell changes did not indicate damage—and that the livers would return to normal. The *Times*, it seemed to me, reflected the FDA's attitude, which I've interpreted to be that they wanted the THA study to fail.

A month or two later, the FDA and Warner-Lambert and the NIA resumed the major testing of THA, which is to last two or three years. I can only say that if I were again to face the problem of an Alzheimer's loved one, I would watch this test like a hawk. I would also watch a similar test being conducted in Canada. And if, after several months, the THA tests showed some evidence of help to the patients, without serious side effects, I would move heaven and earth to force the FDA to make the drug available to all Alzheimer's victims who wanted it, for they are terminal.

Pleased at Jane's responses in the double-blind study, I got her ready to move to the Lawrenceville Nursing Home. For the six weeks of the double-blind test I'd been paying $85 a day to hold the bed at Lawrenceville. It was expensive, perhaps a waste—but what else could I do? And I understood. Homes ran on budgets and they, like any other enterprise, had to have steady income to maintain facilities, staff, and amenities.

I began to get a feel for how different the Lawrenceville home would be when the activities director, Eileen Doremus, said she'd like to come visit with Jane while she was in the Princeton Nursing Home. In she came, smiling, vivacious, gracious—and Jane began smiling at her immediately. Within seconds, Jane was trying to talk to her and, inside her mind, I'm sure, was making jokes.

The move went off without a hitch. I bundled Jane's clothing into several suitcases, and rolled Jane in her wheelchair to the car, where she walked the few feet to the front seat. We simply left the Princeton home, saying good-bye to a few but without any ceremony.

We were welcomed at Lawrenceville as if we were a long-absent member of the family coming home. To begin with, it's a warm-looking, inviting place. I'd written several memos about Jane's special needs in food and feeding, as well as care. Mrs. Bregenzer made copies, placed them inside plastic covers, and left them for reference in Jane's room.

While I hung up Jane's clothing in a closet, twice the size of that in the other home, aides and nurses came in to chat and get acquainted. Within minutes they learned about Jane's walking, what she seemed to understand, and what she couldn't understand. Jane, it seemed, fitted into the routine almost instantly.

At the new home, Jane and I felt that *they cared.*

"Our theme," said Eileen Doremus, "is the song 'You Are My Sunshine.' We play it every morning." Jane loves it, and keeps time.

Within her first three weeks at Lawrenceville, Jane gained six pounds. I was delighted. What pleased me just as much was the way several nurses and aides went out of their way to come up to me, with smiling faces, to tell me that Jane had gained the weight. Once again Jane looks good. Visitors and staff remark on how pretty and young-looking she is.

No longer do I arrive at the home to find Jane sitting in sopping wet diaper and pants. The staff routinely changes diapers and toilets patients at least every two hours. The difference in nursing homes is remarkable, to me—and probably to those who are concerned about patients' skin conditions.

As part of her morning activities program, Jane undergoes regular therapy. In the afternoons and evenings, I walk her several hundred yards. By now she's walking well, even gracefully, while I hold her two hands or keep an arm around her waist. As we walk along the halls, I'm delighted to see Jane looking into other rooms, cocking her head with curiosity, eager to see what's going on about her.

Best of all, she's talking. While I feed her at the evening meal, Jane spontaneously chimes into the conversation with appropriate responses. Often, when she agrees with something being said, she will quickly murmur "Yes," or "Uh-huh." At other times, she will voice a complete phrase in apt response.

A regular visitor, whose name is Carol Kahny, a former teacher, usually stops to chat with Jane before going on to care for her own mother. One day while she was talking with Jane, she said that Jane clearly and plainly said, "I am happy."

It couldn't last—the orderly, almost tranquil routine we were living. Early in 1988, Dr. Summers received another nasty, offensive letter from the FDA. It demanded more records, more paperwork. Never once, of course, did the FDA seek to find out how well Dr. Summers's patients were doing. They only wanted their bureaucratic paperwork.

At this, Dr. Summers seemed to throw up his hands. He notified all his patients of the FDA's action. Then he went on to give me the heart-stopper: He said he would have to stop serving his Alzheimer's patients and devote all his time to fighting the FDA.

What did this mean to Jane? No more THA? I became frantic, again, at the thought of what would happen to her. And I raged against the FDA—those pontifical, egocentric, ignorant bastards who would willingly endanger my Jane for their own silly, stupid, bureaucratic routines. It simply made no sense, no rational sense.

I sent Dr. Summers the following letter:

February 10, 1988

Dear Bill:

This afternoon Jane smiled at me and said, "I love you."

At dinner, she listened to the conversation at the table. At appropriate times, she uttered precisely appropriate comments, sometimes a word, sometimes a phrase. She was aware, she was participating.

She walks about two hundred yards twice a day.

She responds to the Alzheimer's director's activities.

She smiles and responds to all those who smile and speak to her.

So . . . how can you abandon Jane?

Even more pragmatic, how can you damage your brilliant career and probably harm the rest of your life?

Since receiving your form letter and the attached January 19 letter from the FDA, I've talked to Dr. Alan Lisook, the man who was the specific head of the group that prepared this action. And he, while having no adequate response to my charge that all the letter's points were procedural and had little or nothing to do with the health and safety of my wife, insisted that the letter did NOT stop you from continuing your services to your patients. When I charged that the FDA did not let you recover costs of the drug and staff from your patients, he then shifted the blame to Leber and Katz. So . . . I deeply sympathize with you over this outrageous letter and the feelings it engenders in you.

But I am more concerned about saving you . . . and, in turn, saving your patients, including Jane.

One striking fact sticks out of this FDA letter: Nowhere does it express concerns about the health or safety of your present patients. It's all procedural—all focusing on whether you did or did not "follow the rules and procedures."

And this leads me to probably the single most important pragmatic reason for you not to abondon your patients: You need, and can use, all the help and support you can get. Your patients can provide a great deal of that help and support in the contest with the FDA. If your patients, all of them, can and will attest that they have followed the procedures as best they can and remain healthy, and safe, and BETTER because of THA, this in the court of public opinion and Congress can go a long way toward winning over the prissy FDA's concern about rules and procedures.

But if you abandon your patients, for whatever reason, they cannot continue to support you. If you abandon your patients, which I believe physicians should never do if they possibly can help it, newspaper writers who now believe in you, such as Michael Waldholz, may suddenly become alienated. Objective as they may try to be, writers can never avoid being influenced by their own feelings.

I truly believe that time and history will not only find you great but that you will also recoup the costs of the drug and staff. My accountant does not trust the Rehnquist Foundation to pass on contributions to you to help pay for drugs and support a staff. That's why I'm testing the ADRD to see if they will pass on to you the small contribution I made last year—and which they said they had passed on. If they will, then I will be willing to make sizeable contributions which, in turn, I would direct to you.

Did you know that there is an organization in Washington, D.C., called "Freedom In Healthcare" that has set out to fight the FDA? The primary goal of this organization is to help introduce and enact legislation to curb the powers of the FDA. I suggest that your lawyer in Washington, if he hasn't already, try to find out more about this organization and see if it can come to your assistance. In the meantime, I've made a copy of a brochure I've recently received and am enclosing it for you. I will make a contribution to this organization, too.

There is a significant analogy between your battle with the FDA and the battle in World War II between Russia and Germany: One noted expert predicted, early, that "as time goes on, the side that will win is the side that GAINS friends during the conflict . . . and the one that will lose is the side that remains static or loses friends. . . ." Russia gained friends, and won.

You will win out if, in the battle, you gain friends and supporters. That's why I hope you will see your immediate reaction as destructive to you—and hope you will change so that you will gain friends and strength . . . and win.

Jane has run out of THA. WE desperately need a new supply. . . .

At once I began the job of trying to find a source of THA outside of the United States. Thankfully, George Rehnquist, the retired husband of the first THA patient Dr. Summers treated, was working for all of us. He found several pharmacists in the States who were willing to produce THA capsules—THA is in public domain—and sell it to any physician who sent a prescription.

George also came up with a manufacturer of THA in Canada. I called immediately. Surprisingly, I got the director of research on the line. He was pleasant and wanted to be helpful. But there was a problem. They could sell THA anywhere in the world—except the United States. The FDA, he said, was effectively preventing any sales in the United States.

This research director did give me the name of a firm in England and one in Holland that sold THA to physicians in their countries. Perhaps I would know somebody in those countries who could acquire the THA for me, he suggested.

By this time my rage and frustration were making me ill. Jane still had a small supply of THA. I talked with her nursing home physician. We agreed to cut her dose of THA in half and spread it out. Perhaps this would hold her until I could obtain a supply somewhere.

The memory of what happened to Jane when we cut the drug is awful to recollect. As she did when taking the placebo, she almost immediately began to walk at such a slant she couldn't stand up. She began choking on her food— with terrible, deep coughs that seemed to shake her whole body. With every mouthful I was afraid she would throw up and aspirate into her lungs.

At the same time, I thought I would try the FDA itself. I wrote to Dr. Young, throwing myself and Jane on his mercy, so to speak. I asked why Dr. Summers couldn't continue serving his patients and was there some way Jane could participate in the Warner-Lambert FDA study?

Some time later, I received a letter from the head of that section of the FDA. In unctuous tones, he offered our physician and me a way of participating in THA. He sent a mound of papers, technical procedures for monitoring and so on. They were so filled with busywork, so loaded with restrictions, that I hesitated even to show them to our physician. One restriction was enough to turn me off: Jane could receive no more than 80 milligrams per day—which was less than half what she had been receiving for more than a year. What was their reason? That liver enzymes might change? The FDA itself had proved that the liver would return to normal simply by removing the THA. So what was the danger of giving her the dosage she'd been getting?

I decided almost anything else I could do would be better than joining that FDA program.

About that same time, the *Wall Street Journal*'s brilliant editorial writer, Dan Henninger, produced another in his great series on this problem. In the most objective terms, he provided defenses for Dr. Summers and reported on his successes. He raised questions about the FDA, its procedures and it's motivations.

It was a strong editorial basically calling for a review of, and changes in, the FDA's entire set of procedures for approving drugs for terminal patients.

That very week, an international symposium for scientists from every part of the world met in Springfield, Ohio, to discuss the use of THA for Alzheimer's disease. Dan Henninger went out to cover that conference himself. Those scientists verified Dr. Summers's work, declaring that the results of their use of THA on Alzheimer's patients supported everything that Dr. Summers had reported from his experience. The *Wall Street Journal* and the Los Angeles *Times* reported on this conference—again raising the serious questions of why the FDA was dragging its feet over a drug that could obviously help some 3 million victims in the United States alone.

Just at that time, ABC-TV's "Evening News," with Peter Jennings, did a special segment on the controversy with the FDA, the problems facing patients who had been on THA, the Springfield conference, and what patients faced now. This program focused on Jane and me, giving me an opportunity to say on TV what I had said in a letter published by the *Wall Street Journal*—that Jane, coming to THA late in her illness, still managed some quality of life with the drug. I demanded that she be able to continue. The program was focused on a father who had been able to resume almost a normal life on THA—including playing the game of golf he enjoyed. His daughter expressed her near panic at the thought that now her father would revert to his terribly ill state. The program wound up with a summary of the conclusions from the Springfield meeting.

All of these events seemed to give Dr. Summers courage. He suddenly informed all of his patients of a way to continue serving them. His problem, he said, was being able to have enough money to support staff, and buy the drug, fulfilling FDA demands, without bankrupting himself. If patients were willing to donate $306.25 month, he would furnish the THA and continue his care and monitoring. All of us readily agreed to the program.

We put Jane back on the full dose of 200 milligrams per day at once. And within days—hours, it seemed—she was walking upright, smiling, being aware of everything around her, eating good meals without choking or vomiting. In other words, we were back to where we had been before the FDA lurched its way into such venal, stupid behavior.

The pressure on the FDA from around the nation must have been enormous. For in the summer of 1988, Dr. Frank Young announced a change in FDA policy:

From then on, unapproved drugs that families felt would help their terminal patients could be brought in from other countries—for personal use only. This, of course, made it possible for families to obtain THA from the Canadian manufacturer.

Somehow, the FDA couldn't let well enough alone. For reasons that still remain a mystery—and have stimulated some angry speculation—the FDA early in 1989 declared that THA could no longer be brought in from other countries. No explanation.

In another of its brilliant editorials, the *Wall Street Journal* took notice of this FDA action (for it hadn't been widely reported in the press). Among the reasons speculated upon was the possibility that the FDA and Warner-Lambert were having trouble recruiting Alzheimer's patients for their study. Why? Because families who could get the THA were not going to have their loved ones submit to the placebo routine demanded by the FDA. So, apparently, the FDA was going to bludgeon Alzheimer's victims into its study—and into the placebo part of the program—as the only way these patients could get the THA.

My hatred of the FDA and its bureaucracy continues—and will continue until it acts to save people instead of thwart them.

With Jane back on the full course of THA, we resumed our regular way of life.

We have settled into what seemes to be a comfortable routine. I feel that Jane and I could go on this way for years, perhaps many years. She looks fifteen years younger than her age. Her weight holds at an ideal 124 pounds—which I wish she had weighed when she was well.

Aides and nurses and I all know, by now, the best ways for Jane to live and be as happy as possible. On weekdays, I arrive about four in the afternoon and give Jane her juice and vitamins. Then we walk for perhaps twenty minutes.

By then we're ready for the evening meal, which we usually eat in the dining room with Carol and her mother, Mary.

Now, Jane rarely throws up. Either her body handles the drugs better or we're feeding her in better fashion. She hasn't had a deep choking spell in many weeks.

After eating, I'll wheel her to the front lounge. There I've begun standing her at the glass door. She holds on to a railing by herself. She watches the cars, a jogger now and then, and squirrels. She seems to look forward to standing there, watching the outside world go by.

Sometimes we'll sit in the lounge, my arm holding her shoulders, my other hand clasping her hand. Then we'll head back through the halls to the Alzheimer's wing community room, where we begin to watch the evening news on television. Jane watches intently—I only wish I knew how much she understands.

She continues to recognize me. She can see me coming from a distance. Her smile begins, growing wider as I approach. When I'm close enough, she lifts her head to be kissed. And together we kiss in bunches of kisses, as we have for forty-seven years.

To be sure, she is walking less well as each month passes. She has no balance at all. Yet when I pull her up from her chair, she smiles and grasps me in a big hug. At times she seems to be holding on for dear life. But most of the time she begins to pat me on the back as if comforting and reassuring me.

Always in the back of my mind is the dread of her choking, then aspirating food or vomit back into her lungs. That would mean pneumonia and suffering, at least, and probably death. It could happen to a stroke victim, to Jane, at any time.

As I get ready to leave Jane for the night, with bunches of good-bye kisses, telling her I love her and knowing she understands, Jane turns a serious questioning look at me. Perhaps it's my imagination, perhaps not, but I tend to think she knows that I'm going home—and that it would be natural for her to go home with me.

It's time for me to go home. I'll kiss her again and say, "Good night, sweetheart. I'll see you tomorrow. Okay?"

"Okay," she'll say.

I never thought I'd be lonely—ever. Always, it seems, I have more to do than time in which to do it. I could, I suppose, be out every night to cocktail parties or dinners with friends. But I find that when I come home from feeding Jane her evening meal I'm interested only in reading the papers, reading whatever book I have going, watching sports or some of my favorite programs on TV, writing, playing the piano, listening to Glenn Miller on the stero. Never lonely, I thought.

But now I am desperately lonely for Jane. Perhaps I'm selfish? Maybe my actions make me lonely? I want to be with her.

When I'm alone in the house, now, I often find myself talking to her—about friends, our children, and the funny things they did as boys. Too often I think of all the things I wish I'd said or done while she was well and we were together. At those times, I'll say out loud some of my favorite names for her—"little sweetheart," or "my little gammy mammy."

In all my sorrow, the saddest part to me, I guess, is that life goes on in its infinite detail—and Jane isn't a part of it. No more blue eyes peering out of the covers, in the mornings, and smiling, saying "I love you." No more shopping, writing of checks to pay bills, putting out the garbage, laughing at Victor Borge or Bob Hope, loving her family, planning cruises . . . except . . .

Except, perhaps, in her dreams. When I go into the nursing home in the mornings, now, I often find her still in bed. Sometimes she's daydreaming, gazing at the photos of our family or just looking out of the window. Where are her thoughts? Soaring into the whole world? What is she thinking? Dreaming? Hoping? Re-living?

When I come in after her afternoon nap, I may find her still asleep—and waken her with kisses. She comes awake immediately, eyes clear, saying words and thoughts that surely mean coherent statements inside her mind. Where have her dreams been? Surely, where her dreams have been carrying her, life is easier, less complicated, more orderly—with her family and her friends around her. And who's to say this may not be the more important reality?

Whatever impelled me to do it I'll never know, but the other day I pulled out of the files all the letters Jane has written me through the years, from the time we first knew each other.

I spent hours reading through those letters, and now I know I'll spend many more hours reading them—and re-reading them—even though I'm not much of a backward looker. I wept, but I also laughed at her delightful sense of humor, marveled again at her insights into people and ideas, glowed again at her joy in being in love with me and being my wife.

Shortly after we were married, Jane wrote me this letter:

Darling—my very own husband—I love you so, and darling, you must always love me so too—or I don't think I could even exist. It's our love that's the vital, essential and only really important thing in my life—the thing that makes life a greater joy than it ever has been before—before I met you, that is.

It's about noon, and I'm just bursting with love and pride and happiness and a terrible longing for you.

We've got our feet firmly on the first rung of the ladder, and it's just up to us to keep climbing, no matter what the temporary circumstances of our situation, like being separated with you in the Army. . . .

We'll get to the point where we can do nothing but write on our own . . . that point's beginning to come in sight, darling, you wait and see. . . . You know, darling, what means the most to me in all of this selling of articles? The fact that we're starting out professionally together . . . it's so wonderful . . . so rare . . . the beginning of a writing team. It's something to aim for, darling, and together we'll make it . . . and the joy will be so much richer and deeper and more lasting than it would if it came to either of us alone . . . right?

You know, I've been thinking about this business of communication between people . . . never before have I realized what different languages we speak . . . not you and I . . . but we and many of our friends, yes, and our families. You and I have lived so long, and worked and played so long, with people interested in our work, people who read the same things, thought about the same problems, often along the same lines . . . we became narrow in that mode of living, I suppose even though we thought the world and its ills and joys was our oyster.

This difficulty to reach the same epitome of communication with people here bothers me . . . I realize that it's probably not that at all, but rather the terrible feeling of being without you, you who are my life and with whom a silence or a glance was an exchange of communications holding worlds of meaning.

Several times tonight I found myself with a sentence hanging in mid-air . . . they just weren't listening, weren't interested in what I was saying. And it's not that in itself that bothers me at all . . . It's just what that means, what it signifies . . . to me, it seems to represent, in essence, the terrific problem of communication . . . it's the core of our problem as writers, darling; the really tremendous obstacle of reaching millions of people with diversified lives and interests . . . . You know, darling, we can write for our own pleasure alone and have it worthwhile . . . we can write for a living . . . or even to reach a few people . . . but I hope we can learn to write on subjects, and in the way that will interest and please more than the few . . . . I'd like to think we can someday become able to communicate with the thousands and millions who aren't interested in a single thing that's important to us . . . and at the same time, can keep our own integrity, not resort to superficial devices and subjects simply for mass appeal . . . . Darling, I'm getting all balled up and saying nothing, I'm afraid . . . I'm sort of writing you stream-of-consciousness, typing as fast as I can, not thinking things out . . . but darling, that's the next best thing to having you with me . . . the only thing I have left now . . . please don't worry if, from time to time, you get rather incoherent letters from me . . . and if I sound blue or depressed, don't let that worry you, either. Right now, I guess I am blue, the tears are coming a little, yet at the same time, I'm so happy in our happiness, so proud that we're suffering and living and working together through all this separation, that the blueness and the tears pass away.

Darling, there's probably a million things I've left out that I wanted to get in . . . but the one big important point is: When are you going to be back with me? Hurry, hurry, hurry, so we can taste all those billions of kisses we've been storing up, and oh darling, I love you so, yearn so for the touch of your hand, your mouth, your smile and you all over. Until that time, and so long until tomorrow, from me . . . Mrs. Wirsig, gammymammy and your Jane who loves you to pieces.

All my love, always
Jane

Now, some forty-five years later, I leaned over the railing of her bed to waken her from her nap. I gave her a bunch of kisses.

"Darling . . . little sweetheart," I said, "I read some of your letters last night. They were letters you wrote me soon after we were married. I had to go off to be inducted into the Army, but then they rejected me and I came home. I love those letters, sweetheart. Just like talking to you. I love you."

Jane gave me another big kiss. She smiled at me and said, "I love you, too."

Epilogue

One Saturday afternoon, as usual, I came to see Jane. She recognized me from a distance. She smiled. When I reached her she lifted up her face to be kissed. Then she kissed me back in bunches, as she had for forty-eight years.

We walked a little bit, Jane cocking her head this way and that to see what was going on. Then we had supper. She ate a hearty meal.

I kissed her good-bye to go home for the night. She smiled at me and closed her eyes.

Early Sunday morning, a massive hemorrhage hit Jane's brain. She vomited and then aspirated the vomit back into her lungs. Then pneumonia came on, strong and deadly.

Jane died at 5:30 A.M. the following Tuesday, April 18, 1989.

Our family has established a scholarship fund in memory of Jane at Vassar College to honor graduates who want to enter the field of journalism. Jane regarded the full fellowship she received from Vassar to attend journalism school as crucial to her career.

246

At a memorial service, held a month later at the Henry Chauncey Conference Center on the ETS campus, family and friends, colleagues and admirers, gathered to honor Jane's memory. Among the speakers was our son, Guy, who voiced many of his brothers' thoughts. He spoke in the form of a letter:

Dear Mom:

We're all here to say good-bye. I wish you could see this group . . . . Friends and family and colleagues. So many people respect you, and admire you, and love you.

You might be a little embarrassed by all the commotion. I remember how rare it was that you ever celebrated yourself, or felt comfortable when others honored your accomplishments.

I have just a few thoughts for you now. Jenny and Kate, Lisa and Dan, Karen and Claire all send you their love. And, how we wish you could be here to hold little baby Emily . . . and to enjoy all your grandchildren.

Alan and Paul and I seem to be adjusting to middle age. Alan and I now admit that you and Dad should get the credit for how well Paul turned out.

Speaking of Dad, how can I tell you what an inspiration he has been for us all. But maybe you know that after all.

The best way to close, I think, is to thank you for everything. And just one specific thing, especially. I want to thank you for your gift of expression. I realize how my own abilities were formed by your amazing talents.

So good-bye, Mom. We'll miss you, but we know that

your life was magnificent in every respect. And we will always have all those wonderful memories.

Love,
Guy

Good friends have asked me, "Was the struggle worth it, after all?"

They were trying to be kind, I'm sure, wanting to commiserate with me. It's natural, I suppose, for all of us to search for meaning in what we do, what we think, what we strive for. I sometimes think about that question.

Perhaps it would be normal to be bitter over what Jane and I missed, what we lost. And even the thought of warehousing a disabled person, and "getting on" with one's life, may seem appropriate to some people.

But Jane and I loved every moment of our lives, even the few sad moments. To us, who knew how terminal all life is, our time together was precious. Every tiny thread of living was to be savored, protected, buoyed by everlasting hope.

As I think back, Jane and I had the last thirteen years or so of her illness—of her life—to be together in ways we never otherwise could have had . . . holding hands, walking together, hugging . . . telling each other of our love through our eyes, our kisses, uncomplicated by work at jobs. It was a rare, certainly different, often wonderful dimension. In many ways, I think, we were fortunate.

And when she smiled and said, "I love you, too," yes—oh yes, in the most profound sense, every second was worth it.